FINDING
LOVE

Let Your Heart Be
Your Guide

Paula Peisner Coxe

Sourcebooks
Inc.
Naperville, Illinois

Published by: **Sourcebooks, Inc.**
P.O. Box 372
Naperville, Illinois 60566
(708) 961–3900; FAX: (708) 961–2168

Editorial: Todd Stocke
Interior/Cover Design: Wayne Johnson
Production: Andrew Sardina

Library of Congress Cataloging-in-Publication Data

Peisner Coxe, Paula, date.
    Finding love: let your heart be your guide /
Paula Peisner Coxe.
          p.   cm.
    ISBN: 1-57071-031-7
    1. Love.   2. Affirmations.   I. Title.
BF575.L8P42   1995
152.4'1– – dc20   95–11559
                                                         CIP

Printed and bound in the United States of America
10 9 8 7 6 5 4 3 2 1

To love for the sake of love is being human,
but to love for the sake of loving is angelic.

—Alphonse de Lamartine

DEDICATION

Dedicated to the women in my life who have blessed me with their love, support, wisdom and strength. Most of all to my mother—Elayne Peisner, my aunt Sylvia, my cousins Marion and Anita and my friends—Risa, Darryl, Mary and Susan.

To my dear and beloved husband, Roy, and daughters, Samantha and Francesca, who give my life meaning, joy and inspiration, I dedicate this work.

TABLE OF CONTENTS

CONTENTS

INTRODUCTION

Appreciating the friendships and relationships you have nurtured. Waking up every morning with passion for your work. Seeing yourself as perfect just the way you are. Finding your soul mate to share your life with. This picture of life can be yours. No matter how happy you are with your life, there is always room for more love. Invite more love in your world by embracing the essence of life—that it is only with the heart that one sees clearly. Living a loving life is letting your heart be your guide.

Finding love begins with you. You are the key to unlocking love's magic. The first, and perhaps toughest, step is to take an honest, self-inventory. Do you accept yourself fully and unconditionally or are you a bit too self-critical? Do you too often say, "I'm so out of shape…I don't like my body," "I could be doing more with my life…but I'm too tired," "It seems as though I'll never find my soul mate…I meet men who don't treat me as well as I deserve," "I'm too nice and always get hurt"? If you find you are too hard on yourself, you are just like most of us. Loving ourselves more is the first step to finding more love in our life. This book deals with ways to find more love in your life by contemplating three aspects of love:

LOVING OURSELVES is seeing yourself as perfect as you are in every fiber of your being.

HAVING LOVING RELATIONSHIPS is giving of yourself without expecta-

tions, accepting others and letting your heart lead the way.

LOVING LIFE is living your life—mind, body and soul—with passion, joy and purpose.

Part one begins with looking at yourself and how you feel about aging, your body, other people's joys, spirituality and creativity. Loving ourselves means developing our strengths, uniqueness and creativity. We fill our life with self-acceptance and passion when we love ourselves. We envy less. We smile more.

Once we have come to terms with ourselves and begin to truly like ourselves, we then contemplate having loving relationships. The second section of *Finding Love* deals with our relationships to our family, our mate, friends, romance and giving. We invite love in our life when we learn to give. Giving of ourselves, our time, our heart...being vulnerable and open...giving without expecting anything in return—this is the essence of life. We accept the people in our lives "as is"—with no strings attached.

In loving romance, we let go of the notion that the man in our life should be handsome, a good provider, supportive, attentive, fun to be with and rich. We learn to see with our heart and trust our instincts, letting go of our demands and requirements that he "measure up." Who wants that pressure? And who are we to judge someone else with our internal yardstick? Love accepts. It does not judge. Love appreciates. Love makes it safe to be you.

In the third part, Loving Life, we reflect on how we are living our life. Are we

surviving? Are we so busy with our daily responsibilities that we forget to take time to savor life's magic and beauty? Loving life means living it with passion. We more acutely develop our senses— touch, sight, hearing, taste, feelings. We look at adversity with dignity, for we understand that pain is a life lesson for us to learn from and grow. We know our purpose in why we are here and what our role is to make the world a better place. We appreciate the beauty of nature. We love to learn. We have hope for tomorrow.

Creating more love in our life is a day by day process. There is no magical marker in the road you will come across that says, "Here is Love, turn right." Love is the great intangible. We can sense it when love enters our lives, but we can't touch it. You will know in your heart when love enters. Smiling is easier.

Laughing comes freely. You worry less. Your fears subside.

Love embraces us with all its strength as we treat others with dignity and respect, as we see ourself as a perfect work in progress, as we live our life with purpose and passion. Seeking love is a journey of exploration that is never-ending. With each turn, love reveals its many mysteries. Let your heart be your guide and your journey will be all that you want it to be.

The magic in finding love is knowing that love is already within you. No one person and no material thing can give us love. Love always comes from within. To find love, we must give love. To be loved, we must become a more loving person. There is one simple truth—*the love flows through you.*

There are no coincidences in the universe. You chose this book to read because no matter how much love you have in your life today, you are open to loving more and being loved more. You may be searching for new and deeper meaning to your life. You may be exploring new ways of thinking and experimenting with a refreshed approach to life. Whatever your motivation, may you find value and meaning in the loving thoughts in this little book of love.

I will share with you some of the thoughts, teachings and words of wisdom that have helped me and others to inject more and more love in our lives. May you enrich your spirit and nourish your soul as you evolve, grow and change.

The words and ideas of this book of love are intended as a guide for reflection,

contemplation and inspiration. The book is not intended to be a "how to" text because love follows no set rules. To invite love's magic, your heart need only be open, accepting and giving. Love is an enigma, a splendid mystery worthy of endless exploration.

I wish that you find comfort and joy and that you come closer to finding the love you seek. I hope that you will share your love with the world. As you feel love, give love, and it will come back to you! God bless.

PART I–
LOVING OURSELVES

Coming to terms with our life and the choices we have made. Looking into the mirror and liking what you see. Giving yourself a break once in a while. Patting yourself on the back for the good you do. Knowing your purpose for why you are here. When we begin to truly love ourselves, we are able to let go of fear and doubt. We then let love in our life to gently guide us and keep us safe.

LOVING OURSELVES

Who so loves
Believes the impossible.

—Elizabeth Barrett Browning

You will know them well by their fruits.

—Matthew 7:16

LOVING OURSELVES

Love begins from within. From our first awakening, we walk into the world with a pure and loving spirit. With the support and nurturing of our family, we create our place in the world. Love gives us the wings to fly.

Love is the essence of life. Before we can truly love another, we must first love ourselves. Loving ourselves is perhaps the most difficult thing to do. We know ourselves so well. We are our own worst critic. Maybe you still harbor some of these thoughts:

- I need to lose weight…If only I were ten or twenty pounds thinner

- I could be doing a better job of this or that

- I could be more successful if…

- I should be making more money

- I could spend more time with my children if only...

Now is the time to let go of these hurtful thoughts. When we begin to love ourselves, we reframe self-defeating thoughts. We let go of the "shoulds," "what ifs" and "if onlys." By accepting ourselves as we are, we unlock the door to abundance and love, to the power of the universe. We can start today by being good to ourselves.

To paraphrase the biblical saying, "Love yourself as you would like your neighbor to love you." Developing a positive self-image is simply loving yourself. We worry less. Our fears fade. We realize that we are perfect as we are.

Feeling fear, worrying and being self-critical are akin to walking around with mirrors in front of our soul. When someone

13

talks to us, we hear the words superficially, filtered through reflections of self-doubt. We respond with the "I." We inevitably surmise that they think that "I am not nice enough," or "I am not good enough," or "I must be stupid." In these cases, we respond with reflections of ourselves. Our ego is talking, cluttering our mind, casting a shadow over our heart.

A loving response, on the other hand, is to reach out and forego our focus on self. Understand that people generally speak in terms of themselves. They are often fearful, insecure, unsure. They are more absorbed with their own feelings than yours. They are all too often driven by fear and self-doubt. We need only to open our eyes and ears to know this truth. Let go of the idea that we are being criticized, attacked or victimized. Look at the other guy and try to understand their point of view.

Living a loving life is our heart's desire. To do so, we must start by loving ourselves. By accepting who and what we are, we can then begin to embrace those around us with more ease. Tall, short, brown, black, yellow, white, rich, poor...we are all children of God. Once we truly embrace this thought, we then move forward.

Welcome love by letting go of the past, embracing the present and loving yourself fully and completely. With self-love, we begin to trust our instincts, be open to the possibilities and become a loving person to ourselves and others. The past is over. The present is now. The future is abundant.

There is a time to come to terms with your life, your choices. Why not take this time to have a quiet chat with your soul. Think of the hurdles you've overcome, the challenges you've met. As you recall your successes, give yourself a hug and appreciate your inner strength and beauty. Your resourcefulness and self-initiative are but some of your many blessings. Look at the life lessons you have learned. You are a wise soul. Wiser are we now for having learned from the past.

Loving yourself fully means loving your faults. Many of us can find a million faults. Those wrinkles and laugh lines mark the experiences that have brought you here today. They are your marks of distinction. Maybe you think you haven't done enough with your life. How about looking at the people you have touched and the good things you have done for others? Know that your career success will come in time once you have let go of your fears and need to control. Let go of being so hard on yourself. Try a punching bag instead!

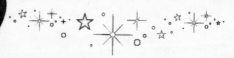

We can think of loving the good times, sunshine and laughter, or we can wallow in fear. Love knows no fear or doubt. It cannot see failure, lost tempers, tummy rolls, mistakes, losses or little wrinkles. Love sees what is essential, which is invisible to the eye.

We are responsible for ourselves and for choosing to live a loving life. Love is a choice. We are all capable of having love in our lives. Yet, having the capacity to love is not the same as having the ability to love. Who best but ourselves to start our loving with?

Loving ourselves is treating ourselves with kindness. Eating healthy, exercising our body, getting enough rest, nourishing our minds, taking time to reach out and give to others, and nurturing our spirituality are some of the aspects of making self-love an everyday part of our lives. Loving ourselves is worrying less and smiling more. We can never laugh too much.

One fine way of creating love is through affirmation. This can be done in silence, in writing, in song, in words. We can repeat meaningful phrases frequently and tell ourselves of the beautiful reality we are creating. We must be able to accept our goodness and know that we are worthy, lovable and perfect. Know that you are beautiful, kind and loving as you already are. Affirm to yourself such loving thoughts as:

- I am worthy of love.

- The more I give love, the more I get love.

- Love works its miracle in many ways.

- I am only interested in loving relationships built on trust and honesty.

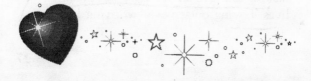

We love our close friends regardless of their flaws; we make allowances for them because of their importance to us, our love for them. Making ourselves our own best friend is the essence of true self-love. Give yourself a break. Love requires time and effort to keep alive. Be kind to yourself. You are your own best friend. Let's start today by making peace with our soul, with our past and with our mistakes. Start by embracing grace in your life and counting your many blessings.

Love can only be found from within. Let's remember to take time to love ourselves.

ACTS OF LOVING OURSELVES

Exercise your mind and body

Replace self-defeating thoughts with "It's okay"

See each wrinkle as the mark of the wonderful experiences in your life that have made you who you are

Meditate and listen to your higher self, relying on intuition for a change

Take one day at a time

Increase your awareness and knowledge of the universe and its powers

Smile when you think a tear is going to drop

Send yourself roses

LOVING AFFIRMATION

I am perfect as I am. I accept who I am,
what I have and where I am going. I walk
with grace beside me and hope before
me. I am thankful for my many blessings.

MY ACTS OF LOVING MYSELF

Giving myself a
hug.
Saying "I love ashley"
Taping a hot shower
+ relaxing.
Its OKAY!
Accepting me

21

MY ACTS OF LOVING MYSELF

_____

_____

_____

_____

_____

_____

_____

_____

_____

LOVING YOUTH

Youth is unending intoxication; it is a fever of the mind.

> —La Rochefoucauld,
> "Maxims"

A warm, cuddly puppy licking your face. A sweet baby cooing with delight. A little child giggling as she swings toward the clouds. Purity and joy are the precious gifts of youth.

The wind against your cheek. The warmth of a big, bear hug. The sound of the chimes blowing in the wind. Remember the first time you felt these things? Everything seemed bigger, brighter, louder. New experiences delight the senses. Being young means experiencing new things.

We can awaken the joy of our senses at any age. Like young toddlers whose mind's eye focuses so well on one thing, we too can learn to block the outside noise and turn our mind's eye to our object of passion. Colors deepen with a passionate view. Things smell richer when we breathe more deeply. Skin

is softer to the touch. Living passionate-ly, leading with our hearts, beckons love in our life.

Youth is innocence. No pretense. The beauty of youth centers in the purity of our spirit. The young heart is pure. Love is unconditional. This reminds me of my three year old daughter who gets so angry when I tell her not to do something that she wants to do because I think she will get hurt. She wails, turns red and kicks up her heels. Five minutes later, she is perfectly fine, wanting to go outside and play. She felt her pain, let me know about it and moved on. Kids hold no grudges. Grownups are more likely to harbor resentment, keep a grudge and not so easily get over being told "no."

There is something beautiful about chil-dren. Something so pure. Who really wants to grow up anyway? Life's more fun lived through the eyes of a child. Heal yourself by embracing the child inside as you journey on love's path.

Finding love of youth starts with yourself. Think back to some of your most joyous times, when you laughed so hard you cried, when you felt so loved your heart sang. Don't you want to feel this good more often? Why not turn back the clock today? Feeling young is a state of mind. Let yourself go:

- Ride a merry go round
- Play hopscotch
- Watch cartoons
- Read the funnies
- Be funny
- Take an afternoon nap
- Skip
- Catch tadpoles

- Go to the park and play...play...play

Feeling young is an attitude. We invite passion in our lives when we feel young and alive. It is only with time that our loving thoughts tarnish as we learn to fear and doubt. Feeling young at heart is a state of mind. We are not required to respond to life with doubt and fear. This is but a choice. We soar through life viewing the world through pure and honest eyes. Make love your choice.

Loving youth means loving energy. Doesn't it seem that children have boundless joy? They can bounce a ball, swim in the pool and run around the yard from dawn until dusk. They seem tireless. Their energy springs unharnessed from their spirit. They may physically be tired, but their mind won't have it. They love to play hard and enjoy life. Sleeping only means they are missing something. What sheer delight we can find in sharing such energy!

There are many mature people who have more energy than some kids I know. My uncle, who is in his late seventies, has a tremendous amount of energy. He is always going, doing, planning, moving. He doesn't sit still but for his afternoon nap. He's right there when someone in the family is planning the next vacation. He has a youthful attitude and wants to experience as much of life, people and places as he can in his waking hours. At seventy or at seven, we can choose to energize our lives and lift our spirits. We are never too old. We are here to enjoy life. Smile. Laugh. Breathe in life's joys. Cherish your blessings.

Young people are our future. When we view youth with loving, open arms and hearts, we give the young the free-

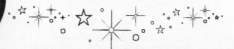

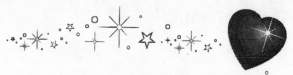

dom to be who they are. Youth means experimenting, learning, dreaming, dealing with new emotions, developing a sense of self. Judging young people harshly unduly constrains their curiosity and passion. It serves no purpose. We can all benefit from being allowed to grow, make mistakes and be true to ourselves.

Much of finding love of youth is feeling young at heart. When was the last time you giggled yourself silly? When did you last climb into a treehouse? Who have you played hide and seek with lately? Playing games and laughing with no purpose but pure enjoyment is wonderfully relaxing and necessary. It's food for the soul. We all can laugh more.

Acting like a child is liberating. Instead of being the perennial parent, why not get down on your hands and knees and color with kids, make funny figures out of *Playdoh*, build your dream house of *Leggos*?

Go roller-blading. Get on a bike. Turn back the hands of time. Imagine. Dream. For nothing exists outside our mind.

Our hearts have a limitless capacity for loving. While we are so busy in our lives, we seem to never have much time to do nothing, relax, laugh, build a sand-castle. Yet, we all are caring, loving peo-ple wanting to break through the demands of our daily lives and enjoy what we have a little bit more.

Life is for the living. Youth is alive. Loving youth is loving life itself. Make feeling young a priority. Make it work for you.

Our children are here to continue our path. With loving hands, we gently guide their way. Embracing the love of their energy and purity, we embrace the beauty of our own inner spirit. We invite love in our life as we open our hearts to youth's divine inspiration.

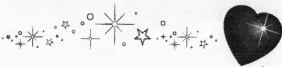

ACTS OF LOVING YOUTH

Build a sand castle

Laugh so hard you cry

Play some games instead of watching the television

Listen to a young person and really try to understand their point of view

Start saying "When I was younger" instead of saying "When I was young"

Look on the bright side

Inject passion into every day

Go play in the park...skip...jump...swing...slide

Listen to rock and rap...understand the lyrics

Teach someone young a lesson you have learned

Go on a date with someone you love

LOVING AFFIRMATION

My spirit is young as I continue to learn life's lessons. I enjoy my life and am thankful for its many blessings.

MY ACTS OF LOVING YOUTH

_____

_____

_____

_____

_____

_____

LOVING AGING

Love is patient, love is kind.
It is not jealous, (love) is not pompous,
It is not inflated, it is not rude,
It does not seek its own interests,
It is not quick-tempered,
It does not brood over injury,
It does not rejoice over wrongdoing but rejoices with the truth.
It bears all things, endures all things.

—1 Corinthians 13:4-7

To many, aging is revered. Older people are considered wise, knowledgeable and learned. They are respected for their experience and ability to teach. The young want to learn from the old.

In our society, aging is a mixed bag. On the one hand, with age, many of us reap benefits: maturity, stability, seniority in our careers, a sense of "mellowness" and wisdom. On the other hand, the physical signs of aging can be worrisome. Wrinkles, sagging body parts, doing things slower or not at all, little aches and pains and greying or balding hair. Some of us slow down mentally with age. We need a little more time to think things over and word things more slowly. Aging comes with its ups and downs.

As the sun sets, it also rises. We will all grow old and die. Aging is a part of life, death the final stage. It is how we

live our life and how we handle the aging process that matters most. If we view ourselves as old, we are old. If we feel young, we are young.

We can see time as a friend, like a soothing bottle of fine wine, aging and increasing in flavor and gusto over time. However we choose to view aging, know deep within our hearts, that time is our best friend, our greatest teacher, our finest healer. It is up to us to believe in time's loving grace.

Finding love of aging is reaching out with acceptance and faith to embrace the inevitable. Many of us find we are happier with ourselves as the years pass. We learn that in our youth, we are often too preoccupied with our concerns, our fears and our needs. With the gift of time, we come to terms with our choices and come to terms with our place on earth.

Our choices change as we get older. What we viewed as options ten years ago are no longer possibilities. Likewise, what we thought was impossible, may now be reality. Like a grand Sunday buffet, life presents its palate of delicacies for our tasting.

Think back on how you felt, what you wanted and where you were ten, twenty years ago? Did you ever think you would be where you are now, doing what you are doing? Probably not. Few of us follow a pre-designed path with no variations. Most of us are swept along by events and desires which cause us to continually re-direct our course.

Our journey on this planet is influenced by our attitude and state of mind. When we see time as a friend, as a valued resource, limited and bountiful, we relish the moment. For all we have is

the present. Love, ageless in its essence, knows no time but now.

If we believe that we are here to be happy, we can be happy at any age. As we grow older, we adorn our face with our life's experiences. Each lovely line marks a wonderful time in our life made up of experiences that contribute to our unique beauty. Look into the mirror and applaud your face, decorated with each and every fine, delicate line.

Love passes through many changes, as does life. What made us happy five or ten years ago, may not make us as happy today. Our needs evolve. Accepting change and the gifts of time are important to loving aging. Know what makes you happy and live your life in the pursuit of happiness. Knowing what you want and proudly wearing a bright smile in your heart makes for happy days and warm nights.

Live today to its fullest. No one has forever. All we have is today. Living our life to its fullest is our greatest reward. We have few regrets. A life unlived is akin to no life at all. Love of aging is rooted in taking one day at a time. When we live each day to its fullest, we are less inclined to fear getting older. We don't let our ego get in the way. We live by the heart.

With time we find peace. In our twenties, we feel a bit like life will go on forever and that we can conquer the world. We are invincible. In our thirties, we are building our lives, making a foundation for our future, nurturing our family. In our forties, we are considering the choices we have left and begin to question our longevity. In our fifties, we come to terms with ourselves. In our sixties, we try to keep it together and prolong our lives. In our seventies, we

try to enjoy every day and make the most of it. In our eighties, we are thankful to be alive. When we are blessed to reach our nineties, we are wondering where all our friends went, when we will visit them and why we are here so long in an ever-increasingly frail state.

At each threshold, love is present. It is up to us to nurture our love, water it everyday and help it to flourish and grow. Love withers and dies if it is not cared for. Treat yourself with kindness. Love the life you live. Let love flourish in your life.

Why not try a lesson in loving yourself? Take out your old photographs and chart the years. Remember the experiences, memories and feelings that each stage of your life has brought. Look at yourself closely: your smile, your eyes, your mood. Ask yourself, How have I changed? What have I learned along the way? What would bring more happiness to my life than anything else in the world? The answers will lead you to where you are today, the best that can be, the you that you wouldn't trade with anyone. Laugh more. Smile a lot. Relax.

Love re-draws the boundaries between reality and possibilities. Things we once thought important tend to pale. Love gives us permission to come to terms with our choices. We try to understand the things we fear. We learn through experience. Know in your heart that aging is a gift of time. Seek to use it wisely.

Finding love of aging is a state of mind. Our attitude shapes our feelings. How many people have you met who seem years younger than their chronological age? They have a gait in their step, a glint in their eyes and a mischievous smile on their face. They have ener-

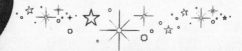

gy. Yet, you probably have come across people who act and look twice their age, carrying the burden of the world on their shoulders. The common denominator is attitude. It is in how we view time, life and ourselves. Aging is one part body and two parts mind.

Know deep within your heart that time is your best friend. Wisdom will guide you through the years as you learn to treat yourself with kindness. First love yourself and the love will come back to you.

41

ACTS OF LOVING AGING

Learn something new everyday

Share your knowledge with someone younger than you

Keep physically and mentally in shape

Be good to yourself

Fall in love all over again

Remember your most memorable experiences and share them with someone you love

Adopt a grandparent

Compile your family history in a lovely album of pictures and stories...remember all the wonderful times

LOVING AFFIRMATION

I look forward to each day. I thank the years for bringing me to where I am today. I open my heart to the teachings of time and the wisdom it bequeaths.

MY ACTS OF LOVING AGING

_____

_____

_____

_____

_____

_____

_____

MY ACTS OF LOVING AGING

_____

_____

_____

_____

_____

_____

_____

_____

_____

_____

LOVING OUR BODY

There is only one happiness in life: To love and be loved.

—George Sand

LOVING OUR BODY

Our body is our temple. It is both sensitive and strong. Our body responds to the world and how we feel about it. When we feel stress, our body reacts. Tight shoulders. Stiff neck. Lower back pain. Our body needs tender loving care, as does our mind, for we are one in body and mind.

Being good to your body means getting enough rest, eating well, exercising and staying happy. Our body reacts in kind. When we treat it well, it treats us well. Our body, when it is content, allows us to do pretty much what we would like. Going for a bike ride, a walk, a hike, a jog. Playing sports. Doing heavy lifting and outdoor work. Our body gives us permission to be good to ourselves and to enjoy life more when we treat it well.

Many of us do not like our bodies. With images of virtual perfection in women like Cindy and Claudia, we can eas-

ily become disenchanted with our appearance. Youth is valued. Aging is not. Clear, tight skin is admired. Wrinkles are not. Flat tummies are the rage. Little rolls are not. Under twenty-five is in demand. Over thirty is not.

We live in a media bombardment of an unrealistic image of the perfect woman. While there is a perfect woman, it is not the image of Cindy. The perfect woman is in all of us. We are all perfect as we are. We are unique. We are human. We are real. We wear our experiences on our face. We carry our genetic markers in our body type. The beauty of each woman is her uniqueness. Every woman is a picture with a story to be told.

Men have it rough too, though not as bad as women. Men are supposed to be hard-bodies, virile, physically active, masculine, yet with a feminine side. How many

men measure up to that? It is virtually impossible. As with women, every man is uniquely beautiful. Men are allowed to wear their experiences on their face. We find greying hair, a bald spot, a tummy tire, and laugh lines can be endearing marks of distinction.

When we realize that we are perfect as we are, it is easier to accept and like what we have been given. Trying to be something or someone you are not is futile. For years I wanted to have blonde hair and blue eyes. I thought that I would be prettier and more desirable. Most of the models, actresses and Miss Americas were.

I thought I was too exotic with my dark hair and dark brown eyes. I could pass for Italian or Spanish anytime. In fact, when I was twenty I was in Spain. One day several people were chasing after

me shouting, "Marchella, Marchella!"
Unbeknownst to me, I strongly resem-
bled a popular Spanish singer. These
people wanted my autograph. Somehow
it became fun to be exotic looking. My
husband, who does have blonde hair
and blue eyes, thinks dark-colored people are fascinating. He grew up in
Florida where being blonde and blue-
eyed was all too common.

Now in my thirties, I have come to
terms with my looks. I'm not so bad and
on a good day can be quite attractive.
But you still can't catch me in a bathing
suit. I admire the women who don't care
that they have a roll or a blob of cel-
lulite clinging to their thigh in plain
view as they meander to their chaise
lounge by the pool. I applaud them. I am
working on getting there. It's funny,
because we may all know the things we
need to do on an intellectual level, yet
on an emotional level we are still stuck.

Love of body is something I am proudly working on this very day.

Share your body. Express your love. Physical love is well-being evoked through touch and demonstration of how we feel. A generous, big hug is worth its weight in gold, especially at the right time. A warm arm around your shoulder. A sincere and delicious kiss. An accepting embrace. These are but a few dimensions of demonstrating physical love through touch, through the skin. In its most intimate form, when physical love is shared between two people, there is a wondrous sense of satisfaction and sharing.

The physical aspect of love is complicated. It is as much ruled by our head as by our heart. We find comfort in touching and being touched. Yet, the purest expression of physical love requires no judgment. Only love.

Take a little self-inventory and be kind to yourself. Look in the mirror in the privacy of your home and scan your body. Start at the top with your hair. Soft, shiny, lush hair is healthy. Do you treat your hair well? Conditioning it weekly is a good idea. Giving your scalp a luxurious massage is a real treat.

Lower your eyes to your face. Are your eyes bright, well-rested? Do you have a twinkle in them? Look at your mouth, your smile. Are your teeth white and strong. Look at how your face changes as you smile. Show your character. Mona Lisa is considered one of the most intriguing women of all time. She is imperfect at best. Yet, her smile is mysterious and evokes an exciting interest in the admirer. Greta Garbo was not the perfect image, yet her character and personality painted a picture of an alluring, strong woman.

Now go down to your neck, to your shoulders, your arms. Do you take care of these tender spots? Protecting your skin with moisturizers and sun blocks is essential. Loving your body is caring for it, protecting it.

Scan your entire body now…to the bottom of your toes. Every curve. Every bump. Every line. Enjoy the uniqueness of you. Wear your life proudly. All your experiences made you the person you are today. Coming to terms with your body and accepting it for all its glory is healthy. Be proud!

It is also healthy to want to improve, tone and strengthen your body. Work on getting fitter, better and more beautiful. You are a divine work in progress.

ACTS OF LOVING OUR BODY

Oil your body from your hair down to your toes

Get a fantastic facial…and have your feet massaged

Have a full body massage, in the dark, with soft music serenading you

Take a sauna to purify your skin

Go have a makeover today…for fun

Fast one day a month

Drink lots and lots of water

Sleep well and long

Rest your feet…they carry you all day

LOVING AFFIRMATION

I am perfect as I am.

MY ACTS OF LOVING MY BODY

_____

_____

_____

_____

_____

_____

_____

_____

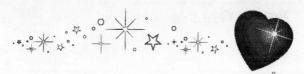

LOVING OTHER'S JOYS

Looking for love is like asking for
a new point of departure...
another chance in life.

—Zelda Fitzgerald

My barn having burned down, I can now see
the moon.

—Zen Koan

Loving unselfishly and unconditionally is pure and honest. Embracing other's successes and joys as if they were your own opens ourselves to the promise of love. We find that abundance multiplies in our own life when we find happiness in the abundance in others. When we feel impoverished and consumed with envy, we invite poverty and illness in our life. We are what we feel. If we feel love, we have love. If we feel lacking in some way, we then find ourselves, in fact, lacking.

We all go through stages in our lives. At one stage, we experience a certain level of emotional and material wealth. When we are in our twenties, we are building our lives. We can choose to see the successful career, the big house, the nice car and the loving family of others as a source of envy or we can see it as a source of joy. Everything has its right time, its right place to enter our lives.

In looking at other's lives, we need remember that nobody's life is perfect. We all have our ups and downs, our joys and sadness. We all look at someone who seems to have the perfect life until we get a little closer. Nothing is as it seems. No matter our station in life, we all tend to live right up to our means. When we look at another's joys with love and compassion, we open our hearts to love and let joy in our own life.

Truly loving another's joys says that we are whole and complete as we are. We are not lacking. The other person's joy becomes our own. There is plenty to go around. One of the most loving acts is to make someone feel valued. Valuing another's life experiences and feelings makes people feel good. When you give love, you get love. Tell someone you care about that you are proud of them.

LOVING OTHER'S JOYS

Loving another's joys comes from the quiet confidence that there is enough success, happiness and goodness to go around for all of us. Find comfort in the knowledge that by giving love, you will receive love. Build your world of love. Start today, one moment at a time, one person at a time.

ACTS OF LOVING OTHER'S JOYS

Celebrate someone else's success

Recognize your friend's good fortunes

Wish others well

Share the joy of a new house or a new baby with your loved ones

Shower love on those who have what you want

Deeply know that there is plenty of love and abundance in the world for all to share

Tell someone you love...I'm proud of you...You are a huge success... Congratulations

Help someone realize their dreams by offering them a job, referral or an open door

Help someone to help themselves

LOVING AFFIRMATION

I rejoice in the happiness and prosperity of others. As I share my love, the universe provides all.

MY ACTS OF LOVING OTHER'S JOYS

_____

_____

_____

_____

_____

_____

LOVING SPIRITUALITY

Spirituality lets meaning flow into daily life.

—David Steindl-Rast

There has been a rebirth of late. More and more people are seeking to understand the meaning of life. We are curious about past lives, about reincarnation. The power of prayer is a phenomena which captivates many. Books fly off the shelf about people who have experienced death and have come back. They tell similar stories, in infinite detail of seeing the light, of communicating with a Higher Power. We are interested in angels, their purpose and powers. We are seeking to find meaning in the here and now and understand where we are going. We are concerned about our own mortality. We want to live with less fear and more love. We want to be at peace.

In our search for answers to life's mysteries, we inevitably turn to exploring the spiritual side of life. Spirituality relates to life, will and thought, separate from matter. You cannot see it. You

cannot touch it. Finding spirituality in our lives is something we choose to feel. We know it when we have found it. The certainty of the light it casts upon our being is as clear as the summer sun on an August day.

Beyond the emotional love between living beings, we find spiritual love. Spiritual love evokes otherworldly feelings of belonging, purpose and meaning from connection with a power greater than what we know on the material plane. Spiritual love is the wings upon which we fly and conquer new heights of understanding, deepen our relationships and find comfort in knowing that the universe provides all.

Belief and desire drive spiritual love, for nothing exists outside our minds. There is no one kind of spiritual love, nor any right or wrong type. Spiritual love is found in God, Goddess, in a Higher Power, in the Absolute, the Almighty, in Buddha, in Jesus, in Allah, Krishna, Brahman, the Tao, the One or in innumerable other ways. Spiritual love harnesses our belief system in greatness and light which reaches beyond what we find walking on this lovely planet. Spiritual love is all-knowing and requires that we open our minds to the possibilities and surrender all doubt and fear to the powers that be.

Whatever your higher power's name, the love that emanates from the Almighty transforms one and all. Love transcends the material universe. In surrendering to our spiritual power, we set ourselves free, free to create love in our lives, free to heal the human heart.

Finding our own spirituality is a very personal experience. No outside

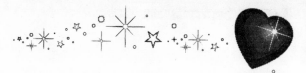

approval is necessary. There is no right or wrong way to go. We journey on our path to spiritual fulfillment alone. While we are connected to the human spirit and to those around us in the world, we are the only ones who can take this journey. Our heart is the guide and our will is the master. We will discover what we need to know.

The journey to understand our spiritual being is endless. As we experience different emotions and gain knowledge of the immensity of our spiritual being, we are humbled. There is no end point. Our journey and searching changes, ebbs and flows, as we expand our ability to delve into the meaning of life, as we open ourselves to the universe and its knowledge. Exploring the spiritual aspects of love places us in an intimate dialogue with eternity. The meaning of our life, the depth of our love, the darkness of love lost and the sheer joy of love present are forces that explore the deepest parts of our being.

There is a calmness and tranquility that overcomes us as we get in touch with our spirituality. It is almost as if the person who has reached a high level of spiritual development sees through all the noise and rises above the material plane. The spiritual being emanates a warm love, a knowledge that what is important is seen only with the heart.

Letting our heart lead our lives is a day-by-day proposition. We all have good days, bad days, ups and downs. Each one of us has our own life stressers that we try our best to keep in check. The spiritually developed person is human too. She works at staying in tune with her heart and letting love lead her life.

To stay physically fit and in top form, an athlete works at conditioning virtually every day. When he slips now and then, misses his workout, pollutes his body with too many bad things, he feels it. He boldly wears the mistakes of the day. Yet, when the same athlete returns to his workout regimen, his state of fitness is immediately enhanced. He looks, feels and performs better.

So it is with the spiritual side of us. Each day is an uncharted marathon, a provocative discovery. When we wake up with loving thoughts and carry them through the day in everything we do and say, we promote living a loving life. As we explore life's unanswered questions and open ourselves to the spiritual world, we experience a building-block of emotions and experiences. Our journey seems to progress, then regress, then soar even higher as we come to under-

67

stand the knowledge we seek, to understand ourselves.

There are many ways to explore the spiritual side of life. Some enjoy reading. New Age books are terrifically popular along with the oldest work of them all, the Bible. Seminars and workshops are another way to explore our spiritual development. Group consciousness can often be enlightening. One-on-one sessions with a spiritual teacher are another form of spiritual exploration. When we find a teacher who can guide us on our own very personal journey, it is as though the seas part, as though we are reborn again and again.

Prayer is a wonderful way to explore our spirituality. We can pray in any setting, individual or communal, private or public. We can use words, thoughts, silence, sighs. We can dream.

Finding love of spirituality takes time. We change and evolve as does love. Nothing stays the same. When we lead with our heart, love lights the way to the ultimate truth—the love flows through you.

Acts Of Loving Spirituality

Pray

Seek to understand spiritual teachings

Be supportive and loving in your comments to others

Meditate

Participate in seminars and workshops involving spiritual development

Recite the Lord's Prayer: "Dear God, may your will be done, on earth as it is in heaven."

Use your talents and abilities to fulfill your life's purpose

Serve others

Surrender to a higher power

Heal the world and yourself by living a loving life

Find the purpose to your life

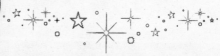

LOVING AFFIRMATION

I live my life in love. May thy will be done, on earth as it is in heaven.

MY ACTS OF LOVING SPIRITUALITY

_____

_____

_____

_____

_____

_____

MY ACTS OF LOVING SPIRITUALITY

_____

_____

_____

_____

_____

_____

_____

_____

_____

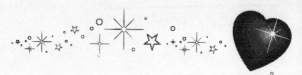

LOVING CREATIVITY

Nobody has ever measured, even poets,
how much the heart can hold.

— Zelda Fitzgerald

How do we find love of creativity? Many think that we are either born creative or we are not. There is nothing further from the truth. We are all creative. None of us think alike. We each see the world differently. We live our lives differently. Yet, we all have the ability to use our intuitive powers to their fullest. Allow yourself to create and you will create.

There are infinite ways to express our creativity, our original thought. In the traditional sense, creativity can be expressed through art, painting, sculpting, music, acting, dance. We can also be creative in how we live our lives. Wonderful, creative dishes can be made instead of thinking that cooking is only a chore. Decorating our environment, our office, our home is a liberating way to express our feelings and desires. We can add flare and originality to how we dress.

We can be creative in our daily work outside the home. In the office, we can look at new ways to do things better, smarter, cheaper. We can find new avenues in dealing with people, in communicating our needs. Like trying on a new hat, we create with a new attitude.

We are most creative in inventing life, in bringing a new life into the world. Our children are our most creative efforts. In creating life, we continue to redefine ourselves. As with life, love continues to redefine itself and passes through many changes. In the child, we find love in its purest form.

Living a creative life is living with passion. A life lived with passion is a life in which love dominates. Love, when left to its own power, creates feelings of joy, peace, security, harmony, understanding, knowledge, comfort and belonging. We create love when we complement one another, when we show appreciation, when we accept and do not judge. The world becomes a better place when we shower our life with love.

I recently saw a wonderful film called "Strictly Ballroom." In it, a young man who has been raised to be a prize-winning ballroom dancer is grappling with his burning inner desire to express himself. In expressing himself, he feels the need to try some new, dramatic steps, straying from the conventional ballroom norm. His desire is portrayed as blasphemous.

He finds a young, inexperienced dancer who shares his passion for new steps and for dancing from the heart. At the end of the film, he has to choose between his heart's creative desire and his ego's need to conform in order to win the grand prize in the dance competition with the traditional ballroom steps.

He chooses his heart. His young, beautiful dancing partner and he dance with passion and fervor, wowing the audience and injecting a delirious excitement through the crowd. The dancers embrace, passionately kiss, eyes fixed on one another as though they were the only two people in the world.

What I loved most about the film was its passion. When the protagonist danced from the heart, he filled the screen and energized the room. It was glorious to see how the heart transcends all when we are true to it. Being true to our heart is leading with love. When we lead with love, we live a loving life.

Finding love of creativity requires us to let go of our ego and listen to our heart. Have you always liked to paint and thought you weren't good enough? Maybe you have liked to write and fell short in your own mind with the little you have put down on paper. Perhaps you have always wanted to start your own business. Maybe you've wanted to give it all up and live on an island selling guava juice. We all have a dream, a story to tell. We all have something to contribute, to make the world a better place. Through digging deep into our most creative self, we can express emotions, thoughts and feelings which heretofore would go unnoticed. Sit down in a quiet place and dream. Let your imagination take you away. Ponder this question:

"What would I do if I knew I could not fail?"

And...do it!

We can experience our potential when we quell the inner critic. We don't need Siskel and Ebert. All too often we

seek outside approval, grasping for someone to recognize us, to like us, to respect us. The truth in love is that a life well-lived is not up for review by anyone but yourself. Only your heart knows the answer.

It doesn't matter if someone applauds, says a kind word or criticizes us. It doesn't change the inherent worth of what we have created. When we truly believe in our heart that we do not need someone else's approval, we set ourselves free instead of setting ourselves up.

Listen to your heart and let it lead you to the path you desire, to fulfill your life's purpose on this planet. So maybe your poetry will not capture the Pulitzer Prize. Who cares? Maybe your poetry will affect lives and make the world a better place. Isn't that more important?

In the last analysis, it is the memories we have created that make life worth living. As Thomas Campbell said, "To live in hearts we leave behind is not to die." Do things of worth and your life will take on a whole new meaning. Be proud to be you.

Let your imagination take hold. Learn to let go and like it!

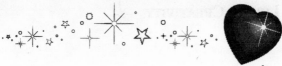

ACTS OF LOVING CREATIVITY

Be Monet for a day

Take your singing out of the shower

Try that new invention on your neighbors

Take up ballroom dancing

Sing off tune

Dance the night away...and wish upon a star

Write the Great American Novel

Invent something crazy

Put on a new attitude

Try on a new hat

Do something joyous and giggle while you're at it

LOVING AFFIRMATION

I am the creator of my soul. I will share with the world my imagination and express my creativity in all I do.

MY ACTS OF LOVING CREATIVITY

_____

_____

_____

_____

_____

_____

_____

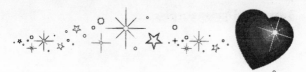

LOVING FITNESS

T'was her thinking of others that made you think of her.

—Elizabeth Browning

Feeling fit is taking pride in your health. Some think that being fit means looking like a bodybuilder or a supermodel. This could not be further from the truth. Feeling and being fit means that you are living a healthy life and taking care of your mind, body and soul.

Being fit affects all aspects of our life. First, we need to get enough rest to let our mind and body have some down time to recharge and rejuvenate. Being fit involves eating the right foods, low in fat and high in nutritional value.

Fitness means exercise. Walking, biking, jogging, working out at the gym, swimming—these are some of the ways we can use our muscles to strengthen and tone our body. Finding love of fitness takes desire. I hear many people who exercise say that they can't stand it. They hate to run. It's boring. Or they

have to force themselves to get up to work out at the gym. Finding enjoyment in sweating and repetition is a challenge.

Fitness to some is like taking a pill which may not taste good, but you know it is good for you. We know we are doing something good for ourselves when we take it. We can do the same with exercise. We can find joy in fitness when we think of the unused muscles and capabilities of our bodies. The more we stay fit, the greater the quality of our life. We can do more and live longer.

The trick to enjoying it is taking it at your own pace. The worst thing to do is to go on a radical makeover plan. Those hardly ever work. Rather, it is best to take a few steps at a time. Try a 20 minute slow walk around the neighborhood. You can graduate to 30 minutes, then to an hour walk. Eventually you can pick up the pace to a light jog.

With eating, you can eliminate some of the bad things in your diet slowly. Maybe stop eating sugar. Or have two pieces of bread a day instead of four. Drink 8 to 10 glasses of water a day to cleanse and purify your system. Try chamomile tea instead of coffee for a change.

Fitness is comprehensive. It envelops all aspects of our being. Fitness is a 24 hour commitment. You can start slow or in one or two aspects of your life. From good rest to good eating to good exercising, fitness is ultimately the grandest act of being good to yourself.

Getting and staying fit takes time. Many of us are the first to say that we can't find the time to exercise. We pick up fast food because we are always on the run and do not have time to prepare a healthy meal. There is a McDonald's

on virtually every corner to tempt us. Love is a greater temptress.

We are inundated with ways to look at fitness from fat grams to calories to our weight to our body fat to our muscle tone. In a dizzying dance with time, when things suddenly have a way of sagging and falling, we race to keep it together, tight and upright.

When we are trying to achieve an impossible dream, we set ourselves up for disappointment. There can only be so many gifts of genetics to go around for thin thighs, high metabolism, fine bone structure. Most of us have got to do the best with what we have. And each of us has a lot of good stuff to work with.

We are all uniquely beautiful in our own way. Each curve to hug and every wrinkle which marks the path of our life experiences possesses a beauty of its own. It is up to us to let our beauty out, to let it shine. Being fit is a sure way to bring out the best in everyone.

Fitness is timeless. It need not matter your stage in life, for at anytime in our life we are able to make a commitment to fitness. Even in our twilight years, we can take a walk instead of just sitting on the sofa. Many people after having experienced heart surgery, find they need to exercise to keep heart muscles healthy. Like never before, they start to walk and have a renewed zest for life.

It is never too late to stop smoking. Studies have shown that once a smoker stops at any age, there is a marked improvement in the condition of their breathing and lung capacity. Quitting smoking is a great way to get fit.

Fitness is also a mental issue. Having a healthy attitude about life is an essential step in keeping a fit body. When we feel confident, hopeful, good about ourselves, we want to do good things for ourselves and for others. Fitness is a way of looking at the world and at yourself with kindness. We treat ourselves kindly when we value who we are.

We can relax our mind and enrich our soul through many types of meditation, prayer, reading, and physical activity like nature walks and tai chi. Taking a sauna can be very relaxing when it comes to clearing our minds and cleansing our souls.

Fitness is a process. One day we may slip and be a couch potato or have a rich dessert. The next day we will run a mile and take two steps forward. The important thing to remember is to take one day at a time. And with each day give yourself a hug for being you, for being good to yourself.

We are all capable of new learning. Whether you consider yourself athletic, thin, fat, in or out of shape, now is as good a time as any to jump on the fitness trail. As a wise saying goes, "Today is the first day of the rest of your life."

ACTS OF LOVING FITNESS

Walk…Walk…Walk

Park farther from where you need to go so you can walk

Eat with nutrition, not your emotions, in mind

Stay active

Rest your mind and relax a lot more

Do a sport you enjoy

Drink lots and lots of water

Meditate

Respect yourself

Build muscles in your body…and mind

LOVING AFFIRMATION

I take care of my body. I respect its power and nourish it everyday through exercise, good nutrition and plenty of rest.

MY ACTS OF LOVING FITNESS

_____

_____

_____

_____

_____

_____

_____

LOVING SOLITUDE

A life spent loving…is a life well-spent.

—P.P.C

We move closer to love as we move closer to ourselves. Quieting the noise in our mind, we find truth in solitude. In solitude, there is nowhere to hide.

Without interruptions, distractions and the outside noise, we are able to touch our soul, our oneness, through solitude. There is a lovely saying that "God mainly speaks in whispers." The whispers beckon to us in the stillness of our mind where we have the space to think deeply, find the truth and know ourselves.

Many fear the thought of being alone. Facing the fear and taking a journey to solitude is the only way to overcome it. Isn't it easier to run around and find something to do, another list to make, another chore to complete, another place to run to? But where are we going? To find love? Likely, we only find more things we feel we have to do in the

pursuit of what is actually doing very little. We come up empty every time, thirsting for a greater sense of satisfaction.

Love comes when it is ready, when we give it space. Love finds the space to grow in solitude. Like a garden cluttered with weeds, the flower that struggles to spread its roots and soak in the sun spends most of its energy just surviving. It has little energy left to produce magnificent blooms. So it is with love. Love needs a clean, clear space to flourish.

Create a space for love in your life today. Make some time to be alone with yourself. Find a quiet, comfortable place. Take thirty minutes and have a chat with your soul. Be silent. Be still. Meditate. Contemplate. Quiet the noise in your mind. You will feel immeasurably rested and refreshed as you bask in the quiet of your private, perfect world.

We often equate stillness with alone-
ness. Yet, in being still, doing nothing,
we do something. We allow the voice of
our inner spirit to speak as we liberate
ourselves from the noise of our daily
lives. Mindless sensory stimulation is
pushed aside to allow us to be at one
with ourselves. Basking in being alone
with ourselves, liking ourselves and
knowing ourselves better is glorious. To
know ourselves is to love ourselves.
After all, if you don't love and enjoy
your own company, who will?

Solitude is a state of mind. Being alone
physically does not address the essence of
solitude. The essence of solitude is in the
psychic and emotional stillness we create
as we open ourselves to the universe.

My deepest and most profound thoughts
come at different times. I often find I am
content and at ease when I am writ-

ing in my little home office, with a soft, instrumental new-age CD playing in the background, the doors open to the cool country air blowing in the room with the sun shining on the green hills of Lake Oswego.

Think about the times you find you are alone, peaceful, contemplating your life. Where are you? What are you doing? Create the moment as often as you need. Revel in your oneness with the world. If you can't go to a serene, quiet place, create one. Close the office door. Put the "Do Not Disturb" sign on your bedroom door. Imagine relaxing on a sun-soaked beach, resting on a powdery sand dune overlooking the sea, the sun benignly warming the air above the gentle waves as they caress the shore. The warm, scented sea breeze blows through your hair.

Now take this picture, transpose the feelings it evokes and store it in a quiet, private corner of your mind. Call upon this picture of serenity as you take the time to reflect, to be still, to be at one with the universe.

When we surrender and let go of our inner noise, we open ourselves to positive thought and energy. The world is full of naysayers, skeptics and critics. In our search for love of solitude, we need to stop ourselves when we begin to second guess, fear the unknown and doubt our intentions. Surrendering to the possibilities allows us to experience our innermost beauty.

Finding love of solitude means we want to be good to ourselves. Making the time to spend with ourselves reaps untold rewards. Taking a walk with the sun at your back, the birds singing

and the gentle breeze caressing your shoulders invites your mind to rest, to relax, to slow down. Being with yourself is ultimate pleasure at its best.

There are many ways to create a state of solitude. Meditation is one of the most powerful tools and allows us to quiet the noise in our mind.

Meditation is liberating, enhancing our awareness and perception. We love more profoundly. We magnify our sensory perception. Meditation focuses the mind's eye on what is essential.

However and wherever we meditate, we surely are better for it. Like the effects of a great workout at the gym, through meditation we acutely exercise our mind and our spirit. Meditation is thought directed by will. It is mastering our self by controlling our mind.

Through meditation, we find serenity. Serenity is a wondrous state of mind. It is the calm, clear way in which we live, think and breathe. Serenity beckons love as its adoring suitor. Invite the joy of solitude in your life. Imagine how you will feel as you worry less and fear no more.

Solitude is a close friend of simplicity. We find the essence of life at its purest form when we live with simplicity. With minimal distractions, our vision becomes clear without the clutter of unimportant things. What is important is only that which is essential. Like unstained, natural wood with its amazingly beautiful and unique grain, lines and shades, we have the choice to marvel at it or to paint over it. When we paint it, we put on an artificial color, which hides the natural beauty of the wood. While it is true that many painted woods are lovely, the

natural beauty of the wood's grain, age and texture remain beneath the painted surface, hidden to the eye. In its simplest form, beauty is in its finest state with the untouched purity and splendor of the natural tree.

Solitude is a place of comfort. It's soothing to quiet the noise in our minds and turn to calm, peaceful thoughts. Feel the fear of being alone, the fear of giving up control, diminish as we enter a state of restful contemplation, as we become one with the world. Let your feelings and emotions flow from within. Your private journey will take you where you need to go.

Some of us are more visual than others and some more auditory. Each of us has a preferred sensory composition. If we are highly visual, perhaps we can best find solitude through minimizing visual

stimulation, lying down, with our eyes closed in the quiet of a comfortable place to contemplate our life and to think deeply. If we are highly auditory, maybe we can find solitude in stillness, with no outside noise to distract us as we reflect, think and rest. We can find solitude anywhere we look. If we need soft music to lull us into submission, then so be it.

Finding solitude does not mean following a single recipe. We can create our own unique flavors in the banquet that is our life. Celebrate you and all that is your life!

ACTS OF LOVING SOLITUDE

Don't answer the phone

Turn off the television for a day...Be with yourself

Do nothing...And don't feel guilty

Take a walk with your soul

Dream in a quiet corner of your mind

Read a wonderful book while wrapped in your favorite sweater

Write daily affirmations to your soul... Be positive...Have hope

Have a conversation for two...with yourself

Take yourself out on a date

LOVING AFFIRMATION

I am comfortable in stillness, in quiet reflection, in peaceful contemplation. In the quiet I can hear my heart sing. I learn. I grow. I embrace the beauty of solitude in my life.

MY ACTS OF LOVING SOLITUDE

_____

_____

_____

_____

_____

_____

PART II– HAVING LOVING RELATIONSHIPS

When we give love, we get love. Having loving relationships starts with letting go of the past. When we create relationships based on trust, honesty and acceptance, there is no room for judgment where love is concerned. Giving love by sharing, listening, caring and thinking creates a circle of love. An outstretched hand. A gesture of kindness. An open mind. Love knows no boundaries where giving is concerned. Love is the greatest gift of the human heart.

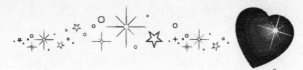

LOVING OUR FAMILY

Believe in love...For it is the ultimate truth.

—P.P.C.

Where you find no love, put love and you will find love.

—John of the Cross

Loving our family starts with forgiveness and acceptance. Forgiveness for what should have been and what never was. It is letting go of any hurt and pain and forgiving. Accepting our parents, brothers, sisters, children and family for who they are, begins with recognizing their unique beauty. Shedding the label of "father" or "sister" allows our family to be themselves without the baggage of expectations attached to who they are because of their relation to you. They are human beings first and foremost, doing their best with what they have.

Most of us can think of many things we would have liked to have happened in our family life that never did. Maybe it was being appreciated more, being recognized more often or perhaps spending more time with our father one-on-one. Maybe it was just hearing "I'm proud of you," "I love you" or "You can do it."

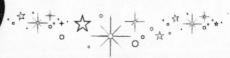

As we know, there is no magic wand. The past is the past. Accepting and forgiving your family allows you to live more fully in the present, just by letting go of the past. Love accepts. Love forgives.

Our family is our sanctuary. Our family holds a place in our hearts where we feel a responsibility for something greater than us. We belong. We are safe. We need each other and are responsible for each other's well-being. We did not consciously choose our parents, nor our other family members. This makes our responsibility even more powerful. Love is a responsibility first and foremost.

I'm reminded of a lovely wedding I attended a few years ago. The bride and groom asked about ten relatives and friends to join them in creating a circle, hands joined together, in front of the other guests. It was a beautiful circle of love. In unison the circle of loved ones recited a statement of loving support for the bride and groom. The circle of love filled the room and touched everyone's hearts.

In today's society, *family* has taken on a new meaning. We have less and less time to spend with one another. More often both heads of household work. And with single parents heading up many households, the pressures multiply. We are pressed for time and have to shuttle around on weekends to do errands, children's sports and party activities—just getting things done consumes most of our time. This leaves us with relatively few precious hours to be with our family...to share...to create memories...to have fun. Remember, love takes time and effort.

Many of us have experienced divorce in our family. I remember how sad I felt

being shuffled back and forth between my parent's houses as a little girl. Ny parents were divorced when I was one year old. Moreover, I lived with my aunt and uncle and their six children until I was six. As loving as my aunt, uncle and cousins were, I was confused, constantly trying to fit in. Most of all I found that my relationship with my father suffered and this psychic pain followed me into my adult years.

My parents were locked in an emotional battlefield. My father quickly remarried and my mother married her work while taking care of me. I was left to find my way. I spent little time with my father, every other weekend visiting him and some weeks in the summer.

It wasn't until I was in my late twenties, having gone through a series of broken, short-lived relationships, that I learned to accept my father in order to be able to accept the love of a man in my life. I had to dig down deep and try to understand that he did his best with what he had. Many fathers spend too little time laughing, playing and creating memories with their children. In *The Merchant of Venice*, Shakespeare writes, "It is a wise father that knows his own child." Wisdom is a choice.

I eventually came to understand that my father, in his own way, loves me. He expresses his love in the way he feels comfortable. That's okay with me. He has been there for me in tough times, with money and good counsel. He wanted me to be independent and be able to take care of myself. He encouraged me to get a higher education. He did what he thought was best for me.

People who hurt us and make us angry are our most important teachers.

Once I came to accept the notion that he couldn't be perfect in my eyes (no one could), I accepted my father. I let love in my life with him and in other areas. As a consequence, I began to have more loving relationships with men. I was no longer looking for the perfect person, for there is no such thing. The world didn't change. I changed how I viewed the world!

Freud suggested that we can follow our psychological road map by following the history of our loves. Our approach to parenting will be similar to the approach we experienced as a child to the extent that we are working out our childhood in our adulthood. I suppose we just keep doing it 'till we get it right.

There is no greater gift than being a mother. The joys of guiding and nurturing a pure soul into the world is a blessing. Our children need us. We are their teachers, guides, supporters and nurturers. Giving them wings to fly with unconditional love allows them to realize their potential. They are free of fear. Children who are loved are able to embrace love in their own lives.

Being a mother is not easy. There is no right or wrong way. Looking back on our own mothers, many of us feel we are better mothers than our mothers were to us. In reality, we all do the best with what we have. Our mothers did their best. When we let go of negativity and criticism for how we were treated by our mothers, we let in love. There is no room big enough to keep love and contempt side by side. Make room for love in your life by forgiving your mother and thanking her for all she has done.

We find love of family through giving. We can express our love through

desire, through wanting to give of ourselves, of our time. Why not take a few moments and think of ways you can create loving experiences with your family? Creating memories warms the heart. Here are a few ideas:

- Send a thank you note, thanking your brother or sister for being there, for just being a part of your life

- Invite your mother and father over for a Sunday brunch and remember the good times on a walk in in the park

- Meet your favorite cousin for coffee and just laugh

- Call a relative you have lost touch with just to say "hello"

- Include your family in your prayers

- Start a family tree of wonderful pictures, stories and memorabilia with everyone adding a personal touch

LOVING OUR FAMILY

Finding love of family comes when we are ready for it, when we have let go of our fears, displeasure at our position and need for approval. Once we accept our mother, father, sister, brother, children and relatives as they are today, we heal ourselves and let go of old wounds. Everything becomes clearer. Suddenly life takes on new meaning. We stop dwelling on the little things.

Loving our family is loving life. Create a circle of love in your life. Begin today.

ACTS OF LOVING OUR FAMILY

Call a relative who you haven't talked to in awhile and see how they are doing

Invite your brother or sister over to spend the afternoon with you

Go out on the town with your parents and be sure to laugh a lot

Lend an ear to those who need you... stop giving advice all the time and just listen...understand

Let them be themselves

Learn a new sport together

Give them something before they feel the need to ask for it

Tell them you love them every chance you get

Count ten wonderful characteristics each of you share in common and smile a lot about it

117

LOVING OUR FAMILY

LOVING AFFIRMATION

I am part of a circle of love. I appreciate
who I am and where I came from. I value
my family and love them just as they are.

MY ACTS OF LOVING FAMILY

_____

_____

_____

_____

_____

_____

_____

LOVING OUR MATE

We love because it's the only adventure.

—*Nikki Giovanni*

When two lives join with a common purpose to spread love and goodness in the world, when two hearts are one, love is created. Implicit trust. Honor. Respect. Loving another is divine. It is why we are here.

John Donne said, "No man is an island." We need one another like the wind needs the sky, the blade of grass needs the soil and the leaf needs its branch. We are one with one each other, inseparable. Yet, it is in the search to find love in another that we run the risk of losing ourselves. Thinking that we will be more complete, happier and somehow better by finding a mate is an illusion. For we are complete unto ourselves as we are. All the peace, joy and happiness we seek are within. Our mind houses our feelings of completeness and contentment.

Finding love of our mate begins with
acceptance—accepting ourselves and
judging no one. In acceptance, we do
not try to change the other person. We
let go of control and relinquish our
power to the power of love. As a line in
"Les Miserables" so poignantly says, "To
love another person is to see the face of
God."

Finding authentic and true love for
another is not about what we can get:
the picket fence, the security, the com-
panionship. Rather, true love rests with
what we can give. In giving, love flour-
ishes. Let love flourish in your life.
There is magic in loving and in being
loved.

Many of us have been through love lost
and forgotten the beauty that beckons
when love arrives and makes its place in
our hearts. We walk through our relationships, intoxicated by the mindless

rumba of romance. Needless to say, these relationships go nowhere, and fast. <u>Love needs to be respected, to be appreciated.</u>

We have the power to take control of our hearts. <u>We gain control by letting go.</u> For love comes when we aren't looking. Like a beautiful butterfly, it softly sits on your shoulder when you turn your attention to other things. By living our life fully, honestly and openly, we invite love to enter. We are ready. We are no longer needy, demanding or afraid. We are content and at peace. Only then can we <u>give love a place to flourish.</u>

Love is a never-ending process. Once you find love, your thoughts turn to keeping it, and deepening it. That's okay. Love is work. Nothing good in this life comes too easily. Love takes time and effort. It can too easily fall <u>prey to our ego and get swallowed up in our</u>

pride. Love is an affair of the heart to be closely cherished.

There are many ways to keep love alive. Share your values, talk openly and honestly about your feelings and desires and share your goals for the future. Do fun things together. Create memories. Here are some loving things to do:

- Leave him a single rose with a loving note on his pillow

- Give him a tiny gift hidden in his briefcase

- Plan a surprise getaway for her

- Make a picnic for two

- Share your dreams while hiking in the hills

Prayer is another wonderful way to share love. You don't necessarily need to pray in a place of worship. Our hearts and minds are enough. I find myself praying two to three times a day. Most often, I silently recite the "Serenity Prayer" in the morning and at night:

"God grant me the serenity to
Accept the things I cannot change
Courage to change the things I can and
Wisdom to know the difference."

It is with great wisdom that we lead with our hearts in finding love. Acquiring personal wisdom through growth and change is a choice we make for ourselves. It can happen at any age. The knowledge and understanding that love is a choice is uplifting. It does not matter your status in life, what you have or how you look. As a wise woman once told me, "There is a cover for every pot."

Finding love goes beyond romance. Romantic love resides in our imagi-

nation, in our longing for connecting with a person we find perfect in many ways through our own imaginings and creation. Romantic love is being in love with love. We seem to melt into another world. The beginning of a meaningful relationship often evokes feelings of romantic love where our love seems too good to be true. We are euphoric. He satisfies our every desire and makes our dreams come true. We do not seek to change the other person, at least not yet. We're just thankful that we found each other.

The idea of love to many of us, rests in the romantic love of a couple. We want to believe that romantic love can carry us through a lifetime. We all want to be needed, to love and be loved by another. Yet, this is but one aspect of love. It is the aspect most consciously sought, frequently found, yet the most difficult to maintain.

With romantic love, the energy we put out is trying to pull the other person closer to us…sending flowers, cards, taking a loving interest in the other person, not finding or seeking fault or blame… this is the euphoria of newly found romantic love. It is a product of our imagination, of our dreams.

But, like the power of Cupid's arrow to pierce our heart, love has the power to hurt, the power to make us feel a depth of emotion unlike any felt beforehand. Think back to when you have said good-bye to a lost love, your heart dropping to the pit of your stomach as you silently ached with a pain as searing as a raging fire. Love touches the essence of who we are in a spiritual dance with our soul. Sometimes the dance is on hot coals. Love is a double-edged blessing.

Shared experiences bind lovers together. Going through the good and bad, the ups and downs, draws couples closer together. The intimacy, warmth, dependability and understanding of spending years together is comfortable, easy. Bind your love together with laughter and smiles. Make it last!

Love has the power to transform. We soar in the rapture of love. We become the best we can be. Our senses become hyper-tuned. Feelings of love evoke a kind of intensity and freshness never known before. Hot is hotter. Light is more luminous. Water is purer and more cleansing. Love magnifies all that is good, all that is beautiful. Love feels good.

Love of our mate is a ballet of the heart. We know each other's deepest secrets. We fear not. We entrust our dreams. In

trusting love, we surrender to our true self and to the power of the universe. Miracles take hold.

Creating miracles begins with the love you make.

ACTS OF LOVING OUR MATE

Tell him how much you love him every chance you get...and show it everyday...in every way

Call her just to say you were thinking of her

Tell her how much she means to you...Top it off with a single rose

Find the beauty in his idiosyncrasies

Find the beauty in her quirky ways... and let her know

Let him have the television remote control...and watch his show with him

Let her do her thing

Stop trying to change him

Stop trying to change her

Give of yourself

Do things together that become yours alone to cherish

LOVING AFFIRMATION

I am open to love.
My heart welcomes the embrace of
 true love.
Love knows no fear.
Love does not judge.
Love accepts.
I am deserving of love and all its bounty.

MY ACTS OF LOVING MY MATE

_____

_____

_____

_____

_____

LOVING OUR FRIENDS

Honesty is the first chapter in the book of wisdom.

—*Thomas Jefferson*

LOVING OUR FRIENDS

Friends are gifts we give ourselves. We choose the friends we have. Unlike family which is given to us, friendships are blessings which we bestow upon ourselves. Friends can bring us up when we are down and can help us to believe in ourselves. A good friend is like a warm hug when we need it most.

As children, many of us find friends in school and in the neighborhood. We all have that one best friend who shares our secrets and our dreams. Friends are like fingerprints making an indelible mark on our lives.

As adults, we make friends in different ways, at work, at school, at clubs, playing sports. We may share a hobby with someone that brings us together. I've found that I have made most of my friends in school and at work. It gets harder and harder to keep friend-

ships alive these days with many people travelling and spending longer work hours at the office and commuting. The telephone is a great glue for keeping friendships alive. We may run up a hefty phone bill, but keeping in touch with those we love is worth it at any price.

Making and keeping healthy friendships is work. Who would think that having friends is work? But, it is. We make time, spend hours listening to stories and giving advice, laughing, learning and forgiving. Friendship takes time. It is an investment of the heart.

Friends do not judge. Friends accept and understand. Like with anything in life, there will be ups and downs. Friends are not perfect. They are pure and with good intent. They enrich. They build us up. Think back to your friends through the years, how they have touched you and made you better for having known

133

them. Call upon this warm and loving feeling when you are in need and know that you are loved.

Our friends are different and yet the same. I have three friends who couldn't be more unalike. Yet, in each I find understanding. We have been through a lot, good times and bad. Sharing experiences and creating memories are the fruits of life. Why not call your friends now and tell them how much you love them and appreciate having them in your life? Spreading love creates more of it. There is plenty to go around.

Friendships change over time. When we live close by, it is easier to spend time together. When we share stages in life such as marriage, children and work life, it is easier to relate. Our friendships grow as we grow. Share the chapters of your life with good friends.

An important part of life is renewal. Our friendships are continually redefining themselves as love continually changes. New people are entering and exiting our lives. With each person that touches our lives, we learn something. There are no coincidences. We are brought together to learn, grow and evolve. Sometimes we move on together for a brief time, sometimes for many years. In each relationship, with each set of experiences, we have the opportunity to enrich our lives. It is what we take from each experience and how we use it that matters most.

Embracing love of friends sometimes means letting go of our own problems and concerns. Just being together, talking and sharing fun moments builds friendships that are healthy and strong. Friends should soothe, not loathe. Friends should comfort, not condemn. Finding love of friends starts with our best friend, ourselves. When we are good to ourselves, it is easier to be good to others. Start by being kind to yourself. Send yourself some flowers. Indulge yourself in your favorite feel-good treat.

A true friend acts with truth and honor. A friend is authentic, and in their authenticity, will tell us what we need to know, not what we want to know. A true friend is like a lighthouse facing a stormy sea, protecting us and guiding us with the light of their love and wisdom.

Friends guide us along life's path reminding us to do the right thing. They remind us to be true to ourselves. Thomas Aquinas wrote, "When you would like to change someone's view, go over to them, take their hand and guide them." You should not manipulate, demand, shout or push. Start from where they are, walking in their

shoes, hand in hand. Through loving guidance, we can be persuaded.

Friends forgive. We can all remember times when we have put our foot in our mouth and said things that were hurtful. Maybe it was because of our youth and maybe it was because we hadn't let a lot of love in our life at the time. We usually are able to apologize, forgive and get on with it. True friendships have an inner radar which sees through the hurtful things we sometimes do.

I have some friends I never quarrel with. There is a harmony barrier we never cross. I don't know which type of friendship is more authentic. Some would say the realness of anger is authentic. Others would opt for the respect of harmony as the key to a healthy relationship. The beauty of friendship is that there is no right or wrong. Friendships just work.

LOVING OUR FRIENDS

When we look back at our life, it is the people who we touch and those who touch us that make a difference. Few remember the office, the successful business meeting, the trophy won or the size of our house. We remember those whose hearts have touched ours, family and friends, for friendships never really die.

Making friends is harder as we get older. We are busy with our careers, our family and our personal interests. Yet, we are never too old to make a friend. Friendship is ageless. We can make a friend on a park bench, marvelling at the beauty around us. We can ask a co-worker to lunch and talk about personal interests outside work, getting to know the person on a more intimate level.

Keeping friends takes love and time. Treat your friend to lunch. Send your best friend a glorious bouquet of fresh flowers.

Make any day a Special Friend Holiday. Send your friends thank you notes just for being in your life. Give of the heart and the love returns to you. The word friendship originated from the ancient Teutonic tribal word meaning "to love." Finding love in friendships makes life worth living. Know in your heart that you are worth it. You deserve to live a loving life!

Friends ask what they can do for you, not looking for what you can do for them. The wheel of life turns and with time each person in the relationship returns the favor. We build and deepen our bonds of friendship through giving, not receiving—giving freely, willingly and without expectation.

Look at your friendships today. Count the many blessings in your life. Tell your friends you love them. And remember to love yourself, for in loving yourself you will find your truest friend.

ACTS OF LOVING FRIENDS

Ask "Is there anything I can do for you?"

Make time to do nothing, just be together

Give your friends a party, even if it isn't their birthday

Invite a friend to lunch and pay for it

Write a letter to a friend recounting your most cherished memories

Tell a friend, "I love you"

Make a new friend

Be your own best friend...Be good to yourself

Next time you want to give unsolicited advice...stop...and say, "I'm sure you'll do the right thing...listen to your heart."

LOVING AFFIRMATION

I am blessed by the friends I have. I do not take my friends for granted. May I continue to accept, appreciate, love and nurture them exactly as they are. My heart is open. Their joys are my joys.

MY ACTS OF LOVING FRIENDS

_____

_____

_____

_____

_____

_____

141

MY ACTS OF LOVING FRIENDS

_____

_____

_____

_____

_____

_____

_____

_____

_____

_____

LOVING ROMANCE

Kindness in words creates confidence.

Kindness in thinking creates profoundness.

Kindness in giving creates love.

—Lao-Tzu

We all love romance. Feeling romantic is feeling alive. When first falling in love, our courtship is sprinkled with flowers, sweet surprises, little gifts and candlelight dinners. Our thoughts are consumed with love. We feel like we are walking on air. We can walk with romance every day if we have love in our hearts.

Romance needs to be created, coddled and nurtured. Creating romance is something we can do at anytime in our life. As time passes, relationships tend to settle into the familiar. The excitement of young love and feelings of longing are replaced with the security and comfort of a person we know all too well. Over time we know each other's foibles, weak spots and idiosyncrasies, along with knowing what makes us laugh and where our most vulnerable spots are for tickles. The power of

romance is how it transcends time and place. It can find you anywhere, anytime, anyplace if only you make it so. You are the creator of romance. Make your finest creation today!

Creating romance is appreciating the little things. Romance is found in tiny portions of love doled out by the heart. From something as simple as remembering to say "I love you" in the morning to surprising your love with a weekend getaway to a sun-soaked, secluded beach with no phones. From the sublime to the magical, we can inject romance into our life everyday in every way.

The little moments are what counts. Catching the twinkle in his eye. Knowing the little laugh line you'll spark as you tell that joke he has heard time and time again. Creating romance begins with opening up our senses to romantic gestures and signals. The signs of romance are everywhere. It is only up to us to see them.

Romance can be found in innocence and joy. Flirting is an innocent romantic tango. What about flirting with the person you adore? When was the last time you gave him that coy wink with your head tilted and hair brushed to the side as you provocatively gazed deep into his eyes? Magic is ours for the making.

Romance is a biological ballet of the sexes in which we court, date and mate. Romance is the means through which we nurture our love, softly embrace it, and give it life. Take the time to demonstrate that you have deeply and lovingly thought about someone. Demonstrate your appreciation and affection.

Romance is talking from the heart. Haven't you found an hour or two of

talking honestly and openly with the man you care about intoxicating? When a man is in touch with his feminine side and retains his masculinity, we go into orbit. Many studies show that the quality most often attributed to long lasting relationships is good communication. Touch. Hold. Stroke. Talk. Live life with passion.

One of the most romantic complements I have heard was attributed to the former ambassador to Great Britain, Joseph Choate. He was asked who he would want to return to earth as after he died. Without hesitation, he proclaimed, "Mrs. Choate's second husband."

Living a romantic life takes thought. One of the most endearing romantic gestures is remembering what people like. What is your love's favorite color, music, shirt, shoes, sports team, wine, food?

Know every physical and psychic nook and cranny of his desires. Caress him with your thoughtfulness, your attention to every detail of the fabric of his life. Embrace her with your tenderness.

Romance needs no suitor. Create romance in how you live. Decorate your home with romantic touches like flowers, lace, soft colors, overstuffed furniture, billowy fabrics, alluring lighting. Seduce yourself.

Redesign your closet. Soft, sensual, inviting, feminine clothing can make any woman feel great. A wonderfully generous hat. An alluring neckline. A beautiful brocade pin. A softly falling scarf. Romance is in our imaginings. Imagine the romantic you and create her!

Romance is the magic of the heart. People like to be around positive,

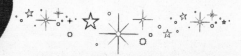

happy people. It makes us feel good. Romance creates a chain of love. We are its links. Faith keeps it strong. Romance is about vulnerability. When we feel romantic, we feel open to love, uninhibited, free, at risk. Take a chance on romance.

ACTS OF LOVING ROMANCE

Dine by candlelight

Perfume yourself like a bouquet of fresh flowers

Let your heart do the talking

Light his fire

Light her fire

Give lots of hugs and kisses

Surprise someone with a loving gesture...flowers, a gift, a night out, a card, a kind word, an embrace

Tell the people you love how much you care about them and show it

Leave a little surprise in his briefcase

Find the magic in his eyes like the first time

LOVING AFFIRMATION

I open my heart to love. I invite romance in my life, in all I do, all I say and all I am. I act with tenderness and kindness decorating my life and the world around me with love.

MY ACTS OF LOVING ROMANCE

_____

_____

_____

_____

_____

_____

MY ACTS OF LOVING ROMANCE

_____

_____

_____

_____

_____

_____

_____

_____

_____

_____

LOVING TO GIVE

YOU

Carress me with your smile

Anything for you

Comfort me with your touch

Anywhere with you

Accept me with your heart

Anytime and all my time

With you.

—P.P.C.

We get back from life what we give. We can give of ourselves, our time, our money. Giving is reaching out to others and to the world with a selfless and caring heart. Giving melts the heart and soothes the soul. In giving, we share ourselves with the world. As the old proverb states: "A sorrow that's shared is but half a trouble, but a joy that's shared is a joy made double."

Some of the simplest acts of giving are the most meaningful. Simplicity and joy are companions of the soul. Just yesterday my cousin called to see how his parents trip to Portland went when they stayed with us for the weekend. The trip was joyous and I will always cherish the time and effort they made to share in our happiness, see our children, our new home and the Pacific Northwest.

At the end of the phone conversation, my cousin, Steve, asked how my mother was doing. I said that her health isn't very good right now, that she is worried and so am I. Without a blink, he asked, "Is there anything I can do?" These simple words brought tears to my eyes. The simplicity, caring and generosity of asking what he can do warmed my heart. Steve is a gerontologist and retirement home administrator. He understands aging and the human heart. I asked him to speak with my mother, just listen to what she is going through. He did so much with six simple words.

We can all reach out our hand to others. Instead of offering advice or trying to solve someone's problem, why not ask simple loving questions like these:

- Is there anything I can do for you?

- How can I help?

- Whatever you need, I'll be there for you. Just ask. O.K.?

Oftentimes the most beautiful acts of giving are found in taking time to listen. It is all too easy to pass judgment, criticize, condemn, offer unsolicited advice and find fault. It is a far richer and purer heart that listens, understands and accepts. Taking the time to listen is a choice. By truly listening, we reach out to the other person, embrace their pain and begin to understand.

True giving expects nothing in return. For, in giving, we share our love, thereby creating more love and making the world a better place. No matter our circumstances in life, we can all give of ourselves. A smile is a gift of the heart. Two simple words, "thank you," can warm the soul. When we give of ourselves and expect nothing in return,

we find we end up receiving more love in other ways.

Giving means appreciating. Think about the many ways we express appreciation. Some tell us how they feel with a word or a card. Some of us don't know how to express our appreciation. Perhaps we feel bad that we can't give back as much. Each one of us is unique in how we express our appreciation. We only need listen with our heart to hear what someone is really saying. "Thank yous" come in many shapes and sizes. Mother Teresa said that there is more hunger for love and appreciation in this world than for bread. How true!

Giving enriches your spirit. Think richly and you will be rich. Think poorly and you will be poor. Nothing exists outside our minds. We project the abundance we are to receive. What we give to the world,

we receive tenfold. Now is the time to reach out to others. Start today by giving of your time, your money, your world.

There are many acts of giving we can do everyday. We can look at what we do not use and give it to someone who needs it more. We can call someone we care about and see how they are. We can spend time with someone we love without looking at our watch. We can give of our time and money to charity to help heal the world.

Maimonides wrote of giving in his definition of the eight degrees of charity. In ascending order, they are:

He who gives grudgingly, reluctantly or with regret.

He who gives less than he should but gives graciously.

He who gives what he should but only after he is asked.

He who gives before he is asked.

He who gives without knowing to whom he gives although the recipient knows the identity of the donor.

He who gives without making his identity known.

He who gives without knowing to whom he gives, neither does the recipient know from whom he receives.

He who helps a fellow man become self-supporting.

Whatever choices we make in how we give, the important element is that we give in any way we can. In each of our roles in life, we give in different ways. As women with many roles—mate, mother, daughter, friend, worker, and sister—we have the unique opportunity to find joy

in giving in the simplest ways during our daily life. Perhaps, as a mother and wife, we make the most personal contribution in healing the world by teaching, nurturing and caring for our loved ones.

Giving knows no material plane. Money does not enter into the equation. It is not how much money or material things you can give. What is essential is the deed, the caring, the outstretched hand you extend to others. My mother, who is retired and living on a fixed income, is the first to give a dollar to a person with their hand out on the street, even though she may only have two dollars in her purse. It doesn't take much money at all to lend an ear and show someone you care. Often, giving is done in silence with only the heart listening. Make every day a day of giving. Start today.

ACTS OF LOVING TO GIVE

Ask if is there is anything you can do for someone the next time, instead of giving advice

Spend a few uninterrupted hours with your friends and family just being together and creating memories

Donate some of your time to charity

Accept and do not judge the next time you feel annoyed or put upon by someone

Choose a smile instead of a frown

Tell someone you care about how much you value them

Give before your friend has a chance to ask for anything

Celebrate your loved ones with gifts...Make everyday a holiday

LOVING AFFIRMATION

I give, and ask nothing in return; for I give of my heart.

MY ACTS OF LOVING TO GIVE

_____

_____

_____

_____

_____

_____

_____

PART III–
LOVING LIFE

Love touches every fabric of our being.
Living a loving life is living with passion
and grace. Soaking up as much knowledge as you can. Enjoying all your God-
given senses—touch, smell, sight,
hearing and feeling. Getting up in the
morning to go to work with excitement
and purpose. Looking forward to a
bright tomorrow. Accepting the people
in our lives and delighting in their differences. Life is like a fresh, spring bouquet of wild flowers to be appreciated
and savored petal by petal.

LOVING THE SENSES

It would be good to find some quiet inlet where the waters were still enough for reflection, where one might sense the joy of the moment, rather than plan breathlessly for a dozen mingled treats in the future.

—Kathleen Norris
"Bread Into Roses"

Warm, rich hot fudge cascading down a generous scoop of melting French Vanilla ice cream. A gentle, tropical breeze caressing your neck as you bask on a sun-soaked beach in the Caribbean. Deliriously dancing on your toes, light as a feather, to the beat of lively Calypso music in a fabulous island hideaway. Hearing the hushed familiar voice of your soul mate as he softly brushes against you tenderly whispering, "I love you...forever."

How do these images make you feel? Delightful, warm, loved...When we awaken our senses, we open ourselves up to uncharted emotional ground. We feel more deeply. We breathe fuller. We walk with a more robust gait. Give yourself permission to feel good.

We are hedonists at heart. Some of us favor different senses; some favor the

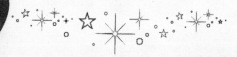

visual, some the auditory, others the sense of touch. Some delight in the tastebuds. Some prefer the sensation of feelings or emotional stimulation. The ability of our senses to create feelings of satisfaction and pleasure is immense. Our senses need to be revitalized. It is natural to want to feel good. Feeling good is healthy.

It is all too easy to forget that we need to feel good. We are more productive, easier to get along with and like ourselves more when we feel good. Yet, we are all so busy doing what is necessary, carrying out our responsibilities in a state of sensory deprivation that we forget to take care of ourselves. While we run about and do more, we often feel less. Our hunger for sensory stimulation is natural and healthy. Passion is the food of life. Bringing alive our senses unlocks the passion within us all. Let passion in your life. You deserve it.

Using our senses plays an important part in finding love. By feeling good about ourselves and our life, we release positive energy. We feel and look great. We carry the radiance of a young girl in love for the first time. We glow like an expectant mother. Our beauty emanates from within. Happy people are attractive. We want to be around them.

Think about the last time you felt really good. When was the last time you were blissfully happy, on sensory overload, where you couldn't take one more moment of stimulation before you'd drop with pleasure? What about the last time you felt pure joy and contentment? It is never too late to feel that good again, to recapture the moment. Take the image you have created and save it in a bright, corner of your mind. Call up the image when you feel you need to focus on joy and let it replace any unwanted feel-

ings that may enter your mind. You create love. It comes from within.

There are many ways we can create love and good feelings by exercising our senses. Try a warm bubble bath tonight, with candles dimly lit, as a soft serenade lulls you into sheer relaxation. Treating yourself to a fantastic CD where the music pulsates as you sip a cool glass of chardonnay while the sun sets, is a sure-fire way to awaken your spirit. Closing your eyes and meditating, in deep thought, as you open yourself up to the images of your mind, allows you to focus on you. Walking through a field of freshly bloomed flowers whose scent overpowers your senses as you deeply breathe its luster, allows you to touch nature and appreciate its beauty. The possibilities are endless. Life is here for us to enjoy…mind, body and soul.

We fully perceive love through all our senses. When we love, we feel transformed. Our senses are magnified. Colors take on a brighter hue. We breathe in richer scents. Our sense of touch warms our soul. A clarity grows around us as the world becomes more in focus. It is as though we can see the universe in a grain of sand.

Love creates pleasure. As little babies are cuddled by their mothers, they produce a chemical reaction. The endorphins rise in the little child. Touch is related to pleasure. There are other hormones, like oxytoicin, which come alive with love. We are chemically linked together in love which can be created by physical and emotional stimuli. The physiological linkage with the spirit and soul is one of life's little imponderables. Love is all-powerful. Love is all-knowing. Don't question it. Surrender to its magic.

We have the power to create pleasure. A hug. A kiss. A smile. A touch. A kind word. Everyday in every way we can create love. Next time you want to say or do something you are not sure of, think to yourself, "Is this a loving thing to say or do?" If it is loving, then so be it. If it is not, then we can make the choice to heal or to hurt. We can say or do nothing. We can say or do something with love. The wise choice is clearly to act with love. In so doing, we create love and we bestow upon ourselves more love. Love heals. Love binds.

The only way to keep love is to give it away.

ACTS OF LOVING THE SENSES

Delight in a delicious, luxurious bubble bath by candlelight

Go get a fabulous massage from head to toe

Give hugs instead of handshakes

Succumb to the scents of a freshly blooming field of flowers

Take a gentle stroll at sunset

Go to the top of a hill and admire the view

Indulge in an indecent treat...topped with loads of hot fudge

Buy the silkiest lingerie you can find

Wear cashmere instead of wool

LOVING AFFIRMATION

I live my life in full appreciation of my senses. In everything I touch, hear, see, feel and taste, there is love. I am the creator of love in all.

MY ACTS OF LOVING THE SENSES

_____

_____

_____

_____

_____

_____

_____

MY ACTS OF LOVING THE SENSES

_____

_____

_____

_____

_____

_____

_____

_____

_____

_____

LOVING HUMANITY

*Our love must not be a thing of words
and fine talk.*

It must be a thing of action and sincerity.

—1 John 3:18

The world is a wonderful tapestry of colors, cultures, lifestyles and customs. Embrace the beauty in life's diversity, for we are all one in spirit. In admiring human diversity and differences, we discover good in all people. Loving humanity inspires an open mind and a singing heart. Now is the time to sing your song.

Since the beginning of time, we have been fighting, culture against culture, religion against religion, race against race. It is a simple task to repudiate someone. On the other hand, we rise above such hurtful behavior and let love's light shine brightly when we rejoice in our differences and appreciate diversity. How sad life would be if flowers did not come in all shapes, sizes and rainbows of colors or if birds did not sing different melodies. We are but one of nature's creations, as different as we are the same when we see with our heart.

We are creatures of habit. Just think about how successful you have been in trying to change some of your tried and true habits. It is hard to change even ourselves, let alone another person. Choosing to respect others and letting them be who they are is an authentic act of love.

While we speak different languages around the world, the language of love is universal. We all smile at the sight of young lovers holding hands, strolling side by side. We knowingly grin at catching a glimpse of couples stealing a kiss on a park bench. It doesn't matter if you are in China or Cincinnati. Love bridges all. Build a bridge of love in your life built on acceptance, tolerance and joy.

Loving humanity may seem a lofty ideal. In the most basic sense, humanity is the collective consciousness of the mortal world. We are all connected as beings sharing a common experience—Life. When something is done to hurt one child, it hurts all children. When a good deed is done, the blessings touch many. In understanding our relatedness to others, we can move about in the world with the knowledge that even strangers are connected to us. Putting a face on humanity makes it real. We are connected to our neighbor, our co-worker, the shopkeeper. We all make up the grand circle of life.

Building a bridge of love between one another makes the world a better place. Is it not just as easy to treat someone with kindness and respect as it is to judge and condemn?

One of the most fascinating ways to find love of humanity is through prayer. There is convincing medical research demonstrating that praying for

someone who has an illness positively impacts the patient, with spontaneous remission and healing occurring in many cases. Prayer nourishes healing.

When we pray, we leave it up to a higher power to let thy will be done. Prayer lets us rejoice in who we are and how we are related to others and to the world. When we open our hearts to a greater power than we know here in the material plane, we are able to find peace and meaning in our lives. It is comforting to know that we are all good and beautiful in God's eyes.

Beauty and goodness are hard to find though. When we watch the television or read the paper, we all too often find sorrowful things…murders, war, crime, poverty. It can be very depressing, if we let it get us down. We have the choice to see that while there is much pain and hardship with many less fortunate than us, we can do our part to continually heal the world and make it a better place. By living a loving life, we make the world a kinder place.

I am continually amazed when I hear stories of kind, generous souls who will see a child in need on the news and then board a plane to try to find and adopt that child. Such generosity of action lifts all our spirits. Each one of us has a generous soul. We need only let go of our fears and let more love in our lives.

Finding love of humanity is a constant struggle with our egos. We want to feel unique and good about ourselves; often feeling good about ourselves is at the expense of others. The easy path is to put down the other guy in order to build ourselves up. This futile attempt at building self-satisfaction pales in the light of

love. There's enough love to go around for everyone. Someone doesn't need less for you to have more.

When we delight in differences, diversity and uniqueness, we are humbled. The mosaic of colors, rituals, customs, languages, dress and texture of humankind is astounding. The heart knows that no one is better than another. The Swede is as beautiful as the aborigine. There is no standard for love. Love accepts all and rejoices in our differences as well as our similarities. By seeking to find the beauty in all that is different, we can more easily let love in our lives.

When we think back across history, many wars could have been avoided, and countless lives saved, if we were able to love our fellow man. Religious-based wars have stood the test of time, with no one winning and everyone losing. In this century alone, literally millions of Armenians, Jews and Ugandans were slaughtered because they were seen as somehow different or tainted. Hatred breeds self-contempt and foretells the downfall of humanity. How lovely the world could be is we hated less and loved more. All we can do is do our part.

There is too much beauty and love in the world to allow hate to flourish. We are wiser for knowing that the real truth of life is found in loving, in keeping love alive every waking moment. When we talk with love, act with love, and live with love, we find inspiration. Our happiness is intensified. Colors, sounds and smells are magnified. Think back to your most loving moments and savor the feelings. Let them linger. Create the picture of the life you want to create. Wiser are we for loving. This sentiment is shared by the Lakota Indians who

absolutely believe that love is the first wisdom, and all that follows is derived from love.

The next time we see someone who is different or who we don't understand, we have the opportunity to find out a little bit more about them. By asking questions, listening and showing interest in everyone's uniqueness, we expand our mind and enrich our life experiences. Through valuing diversity and differences, we gain valuable insights and knowledge. We can start by simply saying, "Tell me more about yourself. I'm interested."

To find love we must walk life's path with an open heart, vulnerable and giving. We let down our psychic armor when we cease to pass judgment, when we accept and tolerate. Finding love of humanity is a choice. When we ask ourselves, "Who would we exclude from love?" we invariably come to the conclusion that everyone has the right to love and be loved.

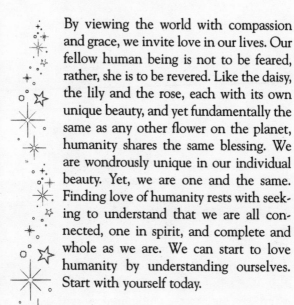

By viewing the world with compassion and grace, we invite love in our lives. Our fellow human being is not to be feared, rather, she is to be revered. Like the daisy, the lily and the rose, each with its own unique beauty, and yet fundamentally the same as any other flower on the planet, humanity shares the same blessing. We are wondrously unique in our individual beauty. Yet, we are one and the same. Finding love of humanity rests with seeking to understand that we are all connected, one in spirit, and complete and whole as we are. We can start to love humanity by understanding ourselves. Start with yourself today.

ACTS OF LOVING HUMANITY

Help out a stranger today

Pick a group of people different from you and write down ten fascinating things about them

Learn a new language

Make a friend with someone different than you

Try ethnic dishes and appreciate the different tastes and aromas

Ask yourself if anyone is better off because you were in their life today

Understand something you fear

185

LOVING AFFIRMATION

We are all uniquely beautiful. We are of the same human heart.

MY ACTS OF LOVING HUMANITY

_____

_____

_____

_____

_____

_____

_____

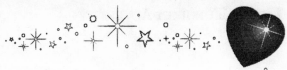

LOVING THROUGH ADVERSITY

One forgives to the degree that one loves.

—*La Rochefoucauld*

Loving Through Adversity

Hard times often bring out the best in us. Our innermost strength is called upon when we experience adversity. We explore new dimensions in our soul. Like muscles we haven't used in a long time, we stretch to accomplish what is needed to overcome, to survive, to make it through.

Adversity is a part of life. In today's trying economic times, many people have lost their jobs or know someone who has. Much of our identities are caught up in our work. We define ourselves by what we do for a living. Losing our job is tough. Know that we grow in times of crisis. Change is a part of life. The clouds will surely part to let the sun shine through. Let faith and hope be your constant companions as you walk the path of life.

Losing someone you love is one of life's most painful moments. Loss has

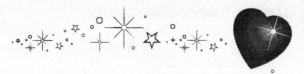

touched most all of us. From losing a love due to the ending of a relationship, to losing a friend because of growing apart, to one of the most piercing losses, losing someone you care about through death. We often find ourselves questioning life's meaning and our future. Know that this too shall pass and love will see you through. Have faith in life's purpose and know there is a rainbow in every storm.

Each of us is sure to experience adversity in our life, for life is made up of the good *and* the bad. Everything changes and change comes in many forms. Sometimes things go very wrong. Bad things happen to good people. When we look at adversity as life lessons to learn from, it is easier to see the blessings in disguise. We undoubtedly grow through pain. We just have to find a way to make it through the tears.

189

The beauty in adversity is experiencing the triumphant power of the human spirit. Haven't we all marvelled at the story of the stranger who passes by a car accident, sees the driver pinned under their car and miraculously lifts the car to save the driver's life? Never before had this hero found such brute strength, yet somehow an inner power took over. We are all heroes. We all have profound inner strength. We need only call upon it in times of need.

Many of us are able to see the rainbow after the storm, the glass as half full instead of half empty and the streak of blue sky above the stormy clouds. This vision is a choice. We choose to see beauty and meaning during tough times and to keep our heads above the surging waters while fixing our eyes on the stars.

It is certain that bad times will befall us all. As the clouds surely clear to a blue sky and as winter turns to spring, sunshine and rainbows will follow. There are miracles in the littlest of things. We can make miracles by empowering our mind's eye to see the goodness in all and know with a quiet confidence that we all have a guardian angel looking out for us.

Reflect on the times when you heard your inner voice protecting you or when you felt a greater power guiding you. Have you ever felt that someone was watching over you? Remember how it feels. Work at building the inner knowledge and confidence that things will work out for the best, that you are safe.

Many of us can think back to when an old love of ours wanted to end our relationship. We thought our world would end. As time crept by, to our surprise, a more fantastic man came along. We had a relationship that was more mature and more meaningful. Love changes. There are no assurances. We only know for sure that love will either grow or die. Love's path depends on us.

Adversity comes in many shapes and sizes. It can be as transient as not having enough money, falling upon poor health, having career problems, harboring unhealthy relationships where we are constantly hurt, to the grandest of all, losing a loved one. No matter its armor, adversity leaves us with an indelible imprint in our souls as we begin to question life itself: Why is this happening to me? What did I do to deserve this? When will my luck change? These questions assume adversity is bad and that we are victims not victors. As victors, we are responsible for our choices and choose our circumstances.

Even in death, we live on. Those we have touched and created memories with are forever etched in both our hearts and theirs. The memories we leave behind distinguish our lives in the grandest of ways. Living a life with love transcends death. Start today by creating memories with those you love.

Remember that at the time we are experiencing bad things, it is hard to see the good that will come out of it. Know in your heart that when God closes a door, a window is opened.

Make a list of ten bad things that have happened to you. Right next to it jot down the silver lining, the blessing in disguise, the thing you learned from it.

In adversity, we find love in pulling together. In our daily lives, we often forget to say "I love you" and show it to those we love. When bad things happen, we miraculously pull together. Wouldn't it be nicer if we didn't need bad things to happen to bring us together? However, adversity shows us that through the self-lessness of love, we rally around the one in need, transcend ourself and focus on satisfying the needs of others.

Natural disasters are something that touch everyone. From the floods in the Midwest to the hurricanes in the South to the Earthquakes in the West, we are all humbled by the power of nature. While extreme in the manifestation of its adverse powers, nature nevertheless illustrates how love has the power to heal.

Let me tell you a story about one of the most amazing things that ever happened to me. My family and I were living in Malibu, California. There had been a series of wildfires burning around

Orange County and in various parts of Southern California in late October. On November 2, 1993, the fire storm wreaked havoc on Malibu. A devastating inferno enveloped the beachside community.

When the fire began to approach Malibu as it blazed through the Santa Monica mountains, I was in Orange County, fifty miles away, at a client. My husband was at his office in downtown Los Angeles about thirty minutes away from Malibu. A call from my aunt alerted us.

I quickly called the babysitter who was poised to run out of the house with one baby, the six month old, in a backpack and the other toddler in a stroller. This was my worst nightmare coming true. I was so far away and the people I most loved needed me. I felt helpless.

Racing down the San Diego freeway with my heart in my throat, I could see the black plumes of smoke over the coastline looked as ominous as an atomic bomb blast. The Santa Monica mountains were covered with a frightening orange blaze of flames. There were people scurrying everywhere, lots of fire trucks racing to the scene and virtual mayhem.

After about two hours of sheer terror, I was able to get to a phone to talk with my aunt. She said that the babysitter and my little girls had called and were okay. They were about one mile south of my house, and a sheriff's car would soon be taking them to me. I had only to wait.

The worst thing was not knowing that the girls were okay. I remember a point when I was pacing in circles at the

gas station figuring out what I should do, when I stopped myself and calmed my mind. A quiet peacefulness entered my innermost thoughts as I reached out to God to beg that my girls be brought back safe. I felt an answer, a warmness embrace me, a calm feeling told me that all would be well. Fear not, for they are protected.

Given the extreme conditions and horror of the time, there was a lot of love created through the adversity of the fire storm. People bonded together and helped one another. Many blessings were bestowed upon us during this horrific nightmare. First of all, we had a babysitter who was resourceful, young and strong, who protected the girls and kept them safe. The most special of blessing was the man who told the sheriff that the babysitter and my two babies were on the beach and needed help. We never

197

found out who that good Samaritan was. Perhaps, he was an angel.

There were more blessings demonstrated in many acts of kindness. Wonderful people helped us: the babysitter, the good Samaritan who flagged down the sheriff, the sheriffs themselves, the sheriff's friend and the gas station attendants who let me use their phone, my aunt who was trying to locate my girls, my cousins who wanted us to stay with them before we could even ask, and the valiant fire fighters who fought the flames from our rooftops on Pacific Coast Highway to save our house.

We received so many calls from friends and family who wanted to be sure we were okay. In such a trying time of adversity, love transcended all. It was very healing. I feel blessed. There are some wonderful souls in the universe.

Our experiences shape who we are. While I look at life differently now, I can honestly say I value life more. I look at things and do not as easily discount it as "not happening to me." I appreciate what I have and try to live my life to the fullest. How differently we would love with the knowledge that everything could vanish in the blink of an eye!

We can all make our love felt while we are here on this planet. A hug. A caring embrace. An empathetic ear. A kind word. A generous heart. An outstretched hand. We have the power to heal both ourselves and others. We can create miracles everyday.

LOVING THROUGH ADVERSITY

ACTS OF LOVING THROUGH ADVERSITY

Help someone in need before they ask for anything

Say "Thank you" to those who do something kind for you

Find a piece of blue sky in the midst of a storm

Look for a window to open when you think a door has closed

Have faith and trust that good will come

Know that "this too shall pass"

Surrender to God and know in your heart with serenity and confidence, "may thy will be done, on earth as it is in heaven"

Know that there are no coincidences… The pain you are experiencing is a life lesson to learn from…Find the meaning in your adversity

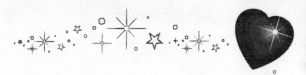

LOVING AFFIRMATION

I know in my heart that this too shall pass. I trust my inner strength to see me through, to find the blessings in hard times. I will always seek to learn from my pain and discover a silver lining in all that is my life.

MY ACTS OF LOVING THROUGH ADVERSITY

_____

_____

_____

_____

_____

MY ACTS OF LOVING THROUGH ADVERSITY

_____

_____

_____

_____

_____

_____

_____

_____

_____

_____

LOVING LIFE

Yesterday is a cancelled check
Tomorrow is a promissory note
Today is cash in hand; spend it wisely.

                                   —*Anonymous*

Love is the essence of life. There are many aspects of love. From the blossoming, romantic love of youth, we are in search of perfect love...dancing to *Love The One You're With*...*You Can't Hurry Love*...*Love Me Tender*...and swooning the night away, we dream of finding our soul mate. Digging deeper, love embraces not only our romantic life, but the spiritual, physical and emotional aspects of our lives as well. Love penetrates, reverberates throughout all we do, all we are.

As we come to learn with time and experience, love can make a positive impact on our work, the way we treat others, how we spend our time and focus our mind's eye, and most importantly, how we treat ourselves. Through love and acceptance of self, we can finally find peace and contentment. We can be happy.

Love is warm, pure, truthful and honorable. Love is packaged in a joyous variety of gift boxes with splendid bows all bound with hugs and kisses. Love is perhaps the greatest gift you can give yourself.

There are many types of love. One of the highest forms of love sought is unconditional love. Profound passages in our lives are often marked with unconditional love showered upon us. We lose our fears to the openness of the heart. Unconditional love is most revealing in the birth of a child which evokes a depth of inspiration unlike any known beforehand. I could never have imagined the depth of beauty and purity in seeing, holding and hearing my newborn daughters as they entered the world.

Unconditional love is inspired in such profound life passages as death, where we forget and forgive any misdeeds. We honor our loved ones who have passed on, wrapped in cherished and tender thoughts and memories. Unconditional love comes straight from the heart. It is glorious, benevolent, kind and so very seductive.

The gift of life is an immeasurable treasure-filled rainbow of experiences. Life is a privilege. We can live it in love or in fear. The choice is ours. Let's let go of the past, stop worrying so much and build hope for the future. Letting go of fear invites love to gently enter your life and take its place in your heart.

Leading a loving life is somewhat of a relief. Somehow what is really important in our lives takes on a deeper and more purposeful meaning. No longer are we as preoccupied with our worries, fears and illusions. We are grounded in the

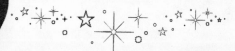

comfort that we are perfect as we are and that life is good. The grey sky always turns blue and the clouds ultimately part to bring in sunshine. It doesn't rain forever. We can walk with a quiet confidence knowing that all is good.

As we have experienced time and again, life does have its ups and downs. There will be illness, death, change, birth, joy, anger, smiles and tears in our lives. Just as the sun sets, it also rises. As summer follows spring and day turns into night, life follows a pattern. We can be sure of change, of good things and bad things happening. By opening our hearts to any and all occurrences, and calmly knowing that all experiences serve as life's teachings, we can begin to count our many blessings. Life's little lessons begin to make sense.

Take a few moments to reflect on experiences that have taught you something valuable. At the time they happened, they may have been painful. But, now with time and wisdom, you can see through the pain and understand the hidden blessings within. With serenity, know that no choice we make is foolish when love is in our life. Everything that happens to us, happens for a reason. We are working out something we have to deal with, emotions that keep us stuck in the same old patterns: bad relationships, jobs we don't like, financial worries. Everything is a stepping stone to get us to our next destination. Turn lemons into lemonade!

All the times we may have gone out with all the wrong men who didn't treat us as well as we would have liked was a wake-up call. We needed to have each experience to teach us that we were going nowhere in that relationship.

Many of us become overwhelmed

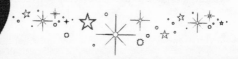

with feeling sorry for ourselves and using the "poor me" strategy. Now is the time to stop being a victim and start making smart choices. The smartest choice is to start respecting yourself and liking yourself as is with no strings attached.

There is always a silver living when love is in our life. We have the choice to see it and believe that it exists. I remember my best friend complaining to me around Thanksgiving about how much she hated her job. Never mind that she always seemed to find a way to not like her job, usually because she thought her boss was not very competent. I said to her, "Well, do something about it." Before she knew it, like a right hook, shortly after she entered a new department, her boss of six months asked her to resign.

She first reacted in shock. She was seven months pregnant and had been with the company for seven years, receiving glowing to good performance reports, raises and promotions. In this new department, she had become persona non grata, a pariah in a sea of sharks.

She didn't seem to know why this was happening at the time. She thought that in the nineties, "This can't happen to me." "This only happens on Oprah," she thought.

So she went about getting a good lawyer who worked out a settlement. No fancy, loud court fights. In the end, she salvaged her pride and boosted her esteem by standing up for herself when something bad happened and she did nothing wrong. She was good and they were bad—and the good guys won. Or so she thought.

She then had to deal with understanding her anger. She dug deep to find

the life lesson, the meaning in why this happened. She came to realize that, to some extent, she wanted it to happen. Her attitude suffered in this new department, yet she still worked her hardest and longest, somehow justifying her poor attitude while managing to keep her clients happy.

While her actions were true to her work ethic, her attitude told a different story. She walked around dissatisfied and would criticize the department and the people. She didn't respect what they stood for and was drowning herself in it. She had to find a way to come up for air, to find some love in all of this.

Through meditation, searching, and personal exploration she found the lessons to be learned. She was able to forgive her ex-boss and thank him, in her own mind, for opening the possibilities. As she had been told time and time again, when God closes a door, He opens a window. The window opening was the jolt she needed to change her line of work and pursue more meaning in her life. She changed careers and is happier. She has forgiven those who caused her pain and has let go of the past. She has moved on. She decided to spend more time letting love in her life.

Many of us have had similar, if not as dramatic, things happen to us in our careers. How did you come through it? I bet you were better and stronger in the end. You had learned a lot and grown through the pain. We must only remind ourselves that there is a blessing in every experience. Count your blessings.

Finding love of life takes time and energy. Keeping it alive is more of an effort, though love's bounty is plentiful

once reaped. We have to work at finding love by shedding our fears. More and more people are afraid of life, of what could go wrong, of what we can't control. This fear, the drama of the ego, mistakes love's true meaning. The ego judges. Love accepts. The ego is protective. Love is vulnerable. The ego holds grudges. Love forgives.

By being true to yourself, you can more easily reach beyond your ego to hear your inner voice, your own authenticity. We learn how to love life, ourselves and others more purely through acceptance. And that acceptance begins with ourselves. Through acceptance we are able to create harmony. As the ancient Chinese and Greeks say, a harmonious life is a happy life.

Reflect on your life for a moment. If you were just told that you had only a few

months to live, what would you do? How would your life be different? What would you change? We all may want to live life a lot closer to our dreams, as though today is the first day of the rest of our life. Make today count. Follow your dreams.

ACTS OF LOVING LIFE

Count your blessings

Say your prayers...two...three times a day

Give something to someone and don't worry about what you get back

Try a little tenderness

Do something you fear

Say "I love you" more often

Smile and laugh as much as you can... especially when you feel like crying

Appreciate ten things of beauty around you...every day

Lead with your heart

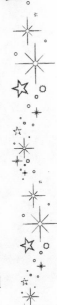

LOVING AFFIRMATION

All of my life's experiences are lessons from which I learn. There are countless blessings in my life which I am thankful for. I will live my life with an open heart and an outstretched hand.

MY ACTS OF LOVING LIFE

_____

_____

_____

_____

_____

_____

Loving Work

To love what you do and feel that it matters—how could anything be more fun?

—Katharine Graham

LOVING WORK

Many of us are caught up in the notion that we are our work. When someone asks, "What do you do?" the first thing that comes to our mind is our job. *What we do is more than just our occupation.* We do a lot of things. We spend time in countless ways. We take care of others. We use our mind to create change in the world. We exercise and do sports to feel good, stay healthy and have fun. We do nothing, in order to relax and unwind. We watch television. We read. We write.

Our life's work is more than the traditional job we have that pays us our livelihood, enabling us to have a roof over our head, provide for our family and realize our lifestyle goals. Finding love in our work is knowing that each one of us has a purpose on the planet. We all have something to do with the gift of life we were blessed with. We all can contribute something of value.

Each one of us may want to ask ourselves why we are here. What unique and special qualities do we bring to the world? When we use our talents and abilities to their fullest, we realize the work we have been set on this planet to perform.

Think about how you are using your talent. Are you using it or letting it go to waste? Share your talent with the world. In this way, you will receive boundless love. When you share love, you feel love. When you give love, you get love in return.

The highest form of work is to serve others, to do our part in healing the world. We are not here solely to sell one more widget, rather we are here to help make people's lives better. Selling (or making) the widget is a means, not an end. Through the daily ritual of selling

219

this widget, we meet many people and have many interesting experiences. Our relationship with people has a purpose. We are here to learn, to teach and to love.

There are no coincidences. In every experience, there is meaning. Our challenge is to understand this simple truth. Maybe we find that we lost our temper with someone and come to learn that now we can choose to react differently to things that don't go our way. Had we not come across this individual, we would not have had our weaknesses exposed. By exposing our frailties, we have the opportunity to learn how to be better at handling adversity, frustration and life in general.

When we live by the Golden Rule, "Do unto others as you would have them do unto you," we are able to share our

gifts with the world with conviction. We are more successful in our work when we serve a higher purpose of making the world a better place. A waitress in a restaurant can see customers as annoyances or can serve to make the world a better place by treating the people who come in with love.

We can all choose to make the world a little better place through our work. Maybe we can be more ethical, more polite with our co-workers or more patient with a new employee, and thereby spread some joy and understanding. Maybe we can just be more honest.

As a young management consultant, I remember a former boss of mine suggesting that the best way to deal with the office politics and egos in the workplace is to treat everyone, from the janitor to the president, as if each person was your client. We want to please our customers and keep them happy. Why not treat everyone with candor, respect and kindness? The world will be a much gentler place.

It is a lot easier to do business with someone you like. People will more readily do things for you and you will do things with more gusto for others when everyone is seen through the same eyes of respect. Every job is important to God. Start today and treat everyone in your work as well as you treat your customers. Say "thank you" more often.

Loving our work means looking at money differently. Money is a reward many of us seek in our work. Finding love of work has nothing to do with money. We can love the work we do and receive millions in psychic gratification and satisfaction while receiving lit-

tle from the Payroll department. Likewise, we may be chairman of the board and earn a million dollars a year, but feel unsatisfied. Money has nothing to do with loving our work.

Why not make a list of all the rewards you find in your job? Rank them and see where money falls. If money ranks high on the list you may not be doing your life's work. Think about what you would like to do even if you were paid half as much. And go do it.

Love doesn't care how much money you have. In fact, an attachment to money, to some extent, detracts from having love in your life. Love feeds on psychic income. Being happy with what you do, with your time on this planet, is the key to finding love in your work. We need only remember that every job is important to God and that our power resides in knowing with confidence that we are fulfilling our purpose on this planet. Count your blessings. Spend your time wisely.

Part of loving our work is valuing the differences in the people we work with. By welcoming different points of view and working with people unlike ourselves, we can gain more complete knowledge. Our decisions are more finely filtered as we listen to opposing views and different perspectives. Differences can be stimulating. Love can be viewed as a constant work in progress, changing, growing, evolving.

We learn to love others more purely by letting them be who they are. Accept instead of judge. Create personal empowerment. People work in a more productive and joyous manner when they feel empowered. Who wants someone

looking over their shoulder or questioning their motives? We want to be trusted, respected and liked, treated fairly and rewarded properly. Creating love in our work means letting people be, letting go of the need to control. Think back to when you felt stifled, like when the boss was always looking over your shoulder. Share what you have learned by being a good example of decency, treating you co-workers with respect and kindness.

Empowerment requires us to welcome the differences and uniqueness in everyone. Just as a bluebird is as different and as captivating as a sparrow, unique in their own natural beauty. We can appreciate the uniqueness in those we work with. We can let their inner wisdom shine and value their differences. How dull the world would be if everyone was the same!

LOVING WORK

Think back to the work which you most enjoyed. Were you part of a team? Were you challenged, respected for your abilities and given the opportunity to realize your potential? Did the people you work with have confidence in you? Liking the people you work with creates a pleasant environment and motivates you to succeed.

Congeniality, cohesiveness and personal empowerment foster abundance. Love of work is easier to find in a supportive atmosphere. And when you get right down to it, we are each responsible for creating an atmosphere of love.

Each one of us can heal the world if only by living a good life, being an example of decency and kindness. No matter what our chosen profession, we can give love and thereby let love in our lives. Love is returned. It is returned in the

little things we do as well as the big things. Everyday we have the opportunity to let love shine. Teresa of Avila said, "Accustom yourself to make many acts of love, for they enkindle and melt the soul." There is never too much love in the universe.

Each of us is gifted. We need only share our gifts with the world.

Acts Of Loving Work

Ask a co-worker for their opinion and really listen

Make every criticism a constructive and motivating one

Treat everyone as well as you would treat your customer

Ask God to please use you to make the world a better place

Be a source of inspiration for someone younger than you

Smile instead of judging your co-worker

Ask what you can give, not what you can get

Do something kind for your secretary today

Take the person you least like in the office out to lunch...and enjoy yourself

LOVING AFFIRMATION

I have a purpose on this planet.

My life's work is valuable as I do my part in healing the world and making it a better place.

MY ACTS OF LOVING WORK

_____

_____

_____

_____

_____

_____

MY ACTS OF LOVING WORK

_____

_____

_____

_____

_____

_____

_____

_____

_____

_____

LOVING
THE MOMENT

Ask, and it shall be given you;
seek, and ye shall find;
knock, and it shall be opened unto you.

For every one that asketh, receiveth;
and he that seeketh, findeth;
and to him that knocketh, it shall be opened.

—Matthew 7:7,8

231

Today is all we have. Yesterday is no more. Tomorrow is but a promise. We receive the gift of time when we are given the precious gift of life.

We can make every moment count. It is all too easy to put something off until tomorrow. Many of us have been known to say, "I'll wait until tomorrow and see...Let me sleep on it before I go ahead...Can't we do that later?" By delaying and postponing, we only end up wasting the time we have.

There is never a better time to do anything than today. A wise old saying rings true, "Today is the first day of the rest of your life." Take this message to heart—today. Live this day with passion as if it were your last.

Embracing the moment is not easy when we are carrying heavy baggage

from our past. Somehow the past sneaks through our veil of happiness and tries to whittle away at our ability to be content and at peace with ourselves. Coming to terms with the past frees us to live in the present.

Many of us are bothered by feelings of guilt for what we have or haven't done, by feelings of regret for what we could or should have done, by anger at feelings of pain and rejection. When we wrap these feelings from our past in a little box and put them in a far corner of our mind, we only then begin to move on. Like a weight lifted from our shoulders, we set ourselves free. Nothing separates ourselves from love but ourselves.

No matter how happy we are, we all live with some regrets and doubts. While it is natural to hang on to regrets and doubts, they only serve to cloud the truth.

LOVING THE MOMENT

Remembering to count our blessings helps us to heal old wounds and move on. We invite light and love in our lives when we stop looking behind us.

Coming to terms with the past is easier said than done. Don't you find that many of us still talk about our childhood or past relationships in terms of what we wished had happened? Still, as adults, we are not able to let go of remaining the child, the victim. Letting go of the past sets you free. We are what we believe. The past is only what we make it. Make the past work for you. Forgive. Accept. Move on.

Living today to its fullest is also a contradiction for those who constantly dwell on tomorrow. The dreamer is seduced by the future, by what will be, what could be, taking into account what is. As the moment slips quietly by, the dreamer is planning the future, all

the while missing today. We would all be wise to keep our feet fully on the ground, living our life in the here and now while shooting for the stars.

Planning for the future and dreaming make life worth living, but not at the expense of enjoying today, for today is all we really have. Living the moment gives us the chance to create memories. Think back on your most memorable experiences. Do you think about some wonderful vacations, times with loved ones where you laughed and smiled, birthdays and holidays spent being together? Our life is a wonderful mix of memories only we create. Understand that we can only create memories in the here and now. We are never too old to experience loving moments.

We are blessed in many ways. When was the last time you counted your blessings?

LOVING THE MOMENT

Why not start right now? Look at where you are today. I bet when you think about it you are pretty satisfied with where you have come, how much you have accomplished and where you are going.

There are many things to be thankful for. Be happy for your health. Hug your children. Caress your husband. Kiss your wife. Appreciate your parents. And, most importantly of all, appreciate being you.

Know in your heart that today's many blessings are guiding lights decorating the path of love in your life.

ACTS OF LOVING THE MOMENT

Buy that expensive toy you have always wanted

Do something good for yourself today

Think deeply about the beauty in your life today

Tell those you love that you love them today—don't put it off

Enjoy your success

Laugh a lot

Smile a lot

Hug a lot

LOVING THE MOMENT

LOVING AFFIRMATION

Today is the first day of the rest of my life.

MY ACTS OF LOVING THE MOMENT

_____

_____

_____

_____

_____

_____

_____

LOVING NATURE

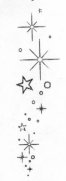

We are born for love,
it is the principle of existence,
and its only end.

—Benjamin Disraeli

239

Nature is that which humankind has not made. There are birds that sing. There are trees that stand proud and tall. There is the sky and its clouds. There is the sea and its sandy shore. There are the mountains and hills of the Gods. There is the barren repose of the desert. It is all for the taking, beckoning us with its allure and magic. Everywhere we look we can find love and beauty in nature. In its purest form, nature's gifts are here on the planet just as we have been placed here—to live, grow and multiply.

Sitting on a park bench, we can devour the beauty around us. Birds are everywhere. Blue, red, brown, yellow. The colors of the rainbow, all in different shapes and sizes. Each has a special sound, a special way of mating, foraging for food and gently gliding through the air. Each sends us a message of love.

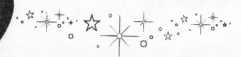

Trees are everywhere. In a tree, we find the root of life. As it grows tall and strong, it builds its branches, provides a home for squirrels, birds, koalas, monkeys and anyone who likes to live up in the air. Tree houses were little private places for us to call home as a child. A swing placed on a generous tree branch delights the imagination. We feel as though we can fly. Trees bring happiness. Trees help us to breathe with the oxygen they provide. Trees are a source of renewal, of strength.

Like human beings, trees are unique in their beauty. A spruce is as beautiful and as different as a rambling oak tree or the monumental sequoia. Each tree is beautiful unto itself. Its bark marks the passage of time. Its leaves change with the seasons. Trees are part of the family of life. Sit under a tree and dream. Sleep. Have a picnic for one. Let its wide branches protect you.

The sky is a lovely place to visit. It never stays the same and always surprises us. The sky decorates itself with clusters of clouds from dozens of different types of big, puffy cotton ball clouds to streaks of ivory-colored pillows that hang suspended in time.

The sky houses a glorious palette of colors. Blues dance on the sun's rays on a summer day. Greys invite our imagination to wander on a snowy winter day. Reds, oranges and yellows lift our spirit as we slow down long enough to enjoy an inviting sunset. Finding love of the sky begins with noticing, appreciating and enjoying its magic. Look up more often. Discover an elephant-shaped cloud, a smiling cloud, a whale cloud. Fly a kite.

Animals in nature abound. From the tiniest creature to the predators of

the wild, animals are a rainbow of God's creations. When we learn to understand their ways and needs, we get closer to nature and its essence. What we seek to understand, we come to love. The heart and the mind are intimately linked in a love dance for the soul.

From the little puppy down the street, to the cat climbing a fence, to the squirrel running up a tree, we have the opportunity to awaken our senses to the magic of nature. We do not need to go out to the wilderness to appreciate the animals around us. Beauty is in our backyard.

Water is healing. The healing power of the ocean, the sea, the river or the lake is nature's prescription for peace and tranquility. Water is soothing. Its sound, its touch, its beauty. It relaxes our mind and calms our senses. Many of us first think to go to the water when we plan our vacation or our weekend getaway. We purify our soul. We enrich our senses. Drink more water. Take a delicious bubble bath. Enjoy a wet sauna. Swim. Float. Laugh in the rain.

The sounds of nature are food for the spirit. Without the noise that fills our lives, we finally hear our true self. Imagine no cars, no horns, no sirens, no screaming voices, no construction work. Now replace the silence with wind, birds, bristling leaves, flowing water, frolicking animals. The sounds of nature cleanse our thoughts and relax our mind. Whether we realize it or not, the noise in our daily life is deafening to our spirit. We soar in harmony with the universe as we appreciate its bounty and pay homage to its power.

Flowers are the pearls of the soil. In each petal there are rainbows. The colors,

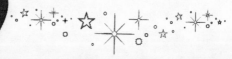

the smells, and the beauty of flowers are unique gifts of nature. Lilies, roses, gardenias, pansies, bougainvilleas—every type of flower is a delicacy for the senses. Flowers fuel a passion in us. We create perfumes to mirror their aroma. We adorn our walls and paint our homes with their color and beauty in mind. We shower our loved ones with them to show we care. We grow and nurture them in our garden to please the senses. Flowers are romantic, alive and magnificent. We feel romantic, alive and magnificent as we appreciate the loveliness of flowers in our life. Buy yourself a bouquet today. Plant a garden. Decorate your soul.

Love of nature is getting back to the basics. Peel back the layers of material wealth. Shed the noise of the day. Finding love of nature is reveling in the simplicity of the earth and our relationship to it. When we seek to become one with nature, appreciate it, and not seek to dominate it, we find the love. Sunshine, fresh air, and fertile soil are the seeds with which we plant the garden of our soul.

ACTS OF LOVING NATURE

Plant a garden

Pick some wildflowers

Breathe the cleanest, purest air you can find

Discover new animals in the wild

Take a long walk in the woods...listen...look...smell...appreciate the sights, sounds and aromas that surround you

Build a birdhouse in your backyard and learn the different songs they sing

Discover playful shapes of clouds above you

Appreciate the sunset...wake early and appreciate the sunrise as well

Take a stroll in the park and count the different types of trees...Try planting a tree

247

LOVING AFFIRMATION

I live in awe of nature, its bounty, its beauty and its power. I appreciate all that is a creation of God.

MY ACTS OF LOVING NATURE

_____

_____

_____

_____

_____

_____

_____

LOVING LEARNING

Dear God, may thy will be done, on earth
as it is in heaven.

—*"Lord's Prayer"*

The mind is a powerful thing. We can will love. We can create love and its demonstrations through being kind, caring, understanding, open, generous and pure. Our mind is our most valuable human asset. Our mind and its thoughts can create a loving life for us or it can destroy any semblance of happiness we may seek. We choose the way we use our minds.

The marvel of the human mind is that we can control it. We can endlessly store new information. We can open our minds to new ways of thinking, to new images. In finding love of learning, we find the means to explore our life and the world around us. In understanding the world and gaining knowledge, we gain immeasurable wealth.

Through learning we can train our minds to understand at a higher level. We

can discipline our mind to suspend any doubts and distractions, to gain the full benefit of our experiences. A sharper focus on life leads to a deeper and better understanding of our purpose and how we fulfill our role on the planet.

Learning is akin to watering a plant. A plant needs nourishment to grow and flourish. So it is with the human mind. The mind needs the water of knowledge. Learning keeps it active, alive and growing. Our mind withers with neglect. Our spirit falters without attention. Through books, teachers and experiences, we have the opportunity to learn and nourish our mind. With a healthy mind, we allow our spirit to soar. Our imagination is ignited.

The important point here is that simply reading a book or attending a seminar or going through a particular experience is not enough. We must want to learn. We need to desire growth and knowledge to truly learn. A teacher cannot teach a child to learn. A child has only to want to learn and the teacher will provide her with the nutrients, the books, the words, the examples.

This reminds me of learning a new language. When I was in high school, we had to take either two years of a language or two years of a science course to qualify for entrance to college. I was inept with the physical sciences and took the path of least resistance, a course in language. I chose French because it sounded romantic.

Needless to say, I did poorly in French. I was not motivated to learn it. I went in jumping over mental barriers to learn how to pronounce words which I never thought I would use again. While I

got a good grade, I did not learn much. I could hardly carry on a conversation or understand a word of a book written in French. "C'est la vie," I said to myself as I entered U.C.L.A., never planning to look back on the land of fashion, art and the Eiffel Tower.

To my surprise, I spent a wonderful summer in Spain visiting friends my freshman year. I fell in love with Spain, the people, the culture, the way of life. I wanted more. So I applied for the year abroad program to spend a year in Madrid at the University. The only glitch was that I needed to take several courses in Spanish to qualify.

Recalling my fear of French, I was nervous about embarking on Spanish, but my motivation was high. This could be the best experience of my life if only I could get through a few quarters of

Spanish. I jumped right in and did quite well. The difference was that my motivation was high. I wanted to live in Spain and needed to speak the language to get by there. I needed to learn it.

The morale of the story is that we only learn that which we are motivated to understand. Learning for the sake of learning is futile. Learning because we want to better ourselves or want to make the world a better place is the real reason we truly learn.

Our mind is a sponge. It soaks up all our life's experiences, records our feelings and imprints our emotions forever. We can call up images and remember what we need to know when we are ready. The mind is our greatest repository.

The wonder of children is that they are always learning. It is exciting to con-

tinually discover another side of life, again and again. Remember the first time you stepped into the ocean, the first time you actually rode a bicycle without falling off it? Like learning to fly, our spirit soars as we climb new branches of the tree of knowledge. The excitement and wonder of a child is ours when we open our minds to learning. A lesson we all can learn, by Mencius, is "The great man is he who does not lose his child's heart."

When we cease to learn, we stifle ourselves. Our creativity is quashed. Our imagination is dulled. Our hopes fade. Fear takes over. When we do not understand something, we often become fearful of it. That which we do not seek to understand, we fear. Learning cracks the barrier of fear and lets in light. We breathe easier as we let in knowledge.

Learning is sparked by listening. When we are talking we are giving out energy.

We do not have much time to listen, to intuit people's reactions. When we listen and really absorb information, we have the opportunity to learn. We learn most when we question. Knowing the answers is a far reach from really knowing anything. Asking questions is the key to gaining knowledge.

I remember when I was working with young, aggressive management consultants fresh from getting their M.B.A. Most of them thought they would show how smart they were by demonstrating they knew all the answers. Often this happened in areas which they were completely unfamiliar with. The really intelligent consultants turned out to be the ones that asked the smartest questions. In an intelligent question, we not only demonstrate our knowledge of the subject, but we also show our interest and ability to deepen our understanding.

Learning is a lifelong journey. We never stop learning about life as we open up, ask more questions and trust in ourselves. Much of our learning takes place on the material plane. We all need to learn certain skills to stay alive, to survive and to prosper. Seeking knowledge on the spiritual plane is a far different challenge.

Spiritual knowledge comes from opening ourselves to a higher power and trusting in its ability to show us the way. As our minds clear, we focus on a higher realm, we are able to heighten our perceptions of the world around us. Not only do we learn to think clearly with our mind, we learn to think openly with our heart.

Thinking with our heart is acting with love. When we process information and deal with people in our lives with a loving heart, we emit energy and create love around us. We can all learn to lead with our heart. We only need to have faith and trust in the outcome to create a legacy of happiness.

We invite happiness in our lives when we understand life using our heart. We intuit higher meaning. We seek to accept, not judge. We empathize, not criticize. We embrace, not reject. We love, not hate. Our heart is the secret lock which unleashes the power of all that is you and all that you will become.

The human mind invites challenge, change and new experiences. It is a muscle which needs to be exercised. We will increase the knowledge in our lives when we open ourselves to learning, to growing and to changing. Change is the fuel that ignites the learning process. New experiences. New ideas. New ways of looking at things. We get better and brighter. The light of knowledge shines on our soul, awakening our spirit and lifting our heart with its wisdom.

Acts Of Loving Learning

Read…read…read

Try something new and ask a lot of questions

Take the opposing view and express it as if it was your own

Understand that which you fear

Gain a deeper understanding of things that interest you

Learn a new trick…and try it out on someone

Ask a lot of questions…without forming the answers

Discover uncharted territory

Take up a new sport

Look up a new word in the dictionary every day

LOVING AFFIRMATION

My mind is open to new things. I will
continue to grow, gain knowledge and
change.

MY ACTS OF LOVING LEARNING

_____

_____

_____

_____

_____

_____

LOVING TOMORROW

Loving yourself
Is loving all
For in everyone,
We find ourself.

—P.P.C.

Hope keeps us alive. When we look forward to the future, we live the present more fully. We know that we are doing things with a purpose in mind. We have a vision, a plan.

Many of us fear tomorrow because it is uncertain. We do not have tomorrow. We only have today. Tomorrow is what we make it. If we think that the future is bleak, that we will be without, then we will surely find a dark day. On the other hand, if we see the future as bright and full of possibilities and new experiences, we will create a happy tomorrow. We create our own happiness through our thoughts and actions. When we will happiness, it sweetly arrives.

In each stage of life, we have a role, a purpose and a mission. Each stage is like a new chapter of a book with the plot unfolding, new characters, exciting

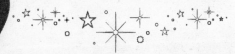

experiences and lots of learning. Life is like a book with many chapters. With each chapter, we live a little more in our creation, our book of life.

One thing is for sure—nothing stays the same. It is also true that you never know what tomorrow will bring. We know for sure that we will all experience joy and pain. We cannot control life's forces. We can only make the choice to deal with life with grace. We can learn from our mistakes or we can repeat them. We can wallow in our pain or we can rise above it and strengthen our resolve. We can take for granted the good things in our lives or we can appreciate and nurture them to keep them alive. The choice resides in our attitude, in how we choose to see the world. When we live a life of grace, love beckons us.

I like the expression "perception is reality." That which exists rests in our perception of it. Imagine waking up one morning on vacation looking out onto the Caribbean. One person may think it is too hot to do anything and stay in the air-conditioned room until it cools off outside. Another person may see the ocean as inviting, wanting to jump in and savor its beauty. Still another may close the curtains and go back to sleep. The morning has not changed. The sea is the sea. The sky is the sky. The sun is the sun. How we perceive these things makes the difference. They can be nuisances, annoyances, sources of joy and pleasure or simply background. We make of life what we want.

Hope is the nourishment that sustains our soul. Yet, sometimes we wait around hoping for things to change. We miss life when we wait for love;. for in waiting for love, we withhold it from ourselves. When we withhold love, we

take the best of what we have and put it on a shelf. Others will never know of the love in our heart when we keep it in abeyance. Living in the present with a view of a hopeful tomorrow, we create our own paradise by letting love in. Create your paradise of love. What better time to start than today.

Love does not stay the same. We can be sure of that. There are no guarantees of tomorrow. Love changes. It grows. It deepens. It also dies. Fearing not, we let love in to take its course in our life.

Thinking about tomorrow, have a gentle talk with your soul. What gives my life meaning? Why am I here? What would make me happy? If I did not fear failing, what would I do with my life? Exploring the answers to these questions is probing into the deep recesses of your soul. Making the changes necessary to get where you want to go is even harder. Take one step at a time. Once you have found your answers, live your life with purpose and confidence, knowing that love will be your loyal and constant companion.

A wise Talmudic teaching tells us that "If one tries to grasp too much, one grasps nothing." It is better to take small steps towards your goal, not leap too far and wide, for with small steps we build on our success and progress. One step at a time. One day at a time.

Some of us like to look at our chosen one and want to change them. Yet, we all know that you can't change someone. Changing someone else is futile. We get nowhere and are disappointed. Loving someone is accepting them, not changing them. Changing implies judgement. Judgement is conditional. Love is unconditional.

The story of Voltaire's *Candide* tells of the futility of wanting to change your loved one. While the lovers are planning their future, the hero talks of wanting a rural life in the countryside. The heroine wants material finery, jewels, manors and comfort. They foolishly expect love to solve their differences. But, as we know, love does not. Love cannot bridge differences created by the ego. The ego is not pure self. Love is pure selflessness.

The simple truth is that we must begin by appreciating what we have and who we are today before we can build a happy, loving tomorrow. We're often in so big a rush getting somewhere, trying to do too much in too little time, that we forget to enjoy where we are.

Why not start with thinking about the many blessings in your life, today?

Think of all the love and joy that is in your life, of all you have accomplished, of all you have become. Think about the many wondrous ways you are sharing this with the world, for as we give love, we receive love in return, in untold blissful ways.

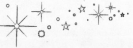

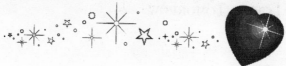

ACTS OF LOVING TOMORROW

Make plans for the future

Give of your time, heart, mind and possessions to build a brighter tomorrow

Walk with confidence in knowing your purpose in life...then fulfill it on your personal journey of love

Ask yourself, "What would I do with my life now if I had no fears?"...And, do it!

See rainbows and sunshine instead of clouds and storms

Make room for change

Forgive the past and move on

Live the present fully and joyfully

LOVING AFFIRMATION

I walk with grace, knowing that tomorrow will be brimming over with joy, prosperity and love.

MY ACTS OF LOVING TOMORROW

_____

_____

_____

_____

_____

_____

_____

SOME FINAL THOUGHTS OF LOVE

I hope that after having read this book you have made a little extra room in your heart to love yourself and the world around you more. My purpose in sharing these thoughts of love is to help make the world a better place by offering insights into how we can create more love in our lives.

Creating love in our life is a day by day, step by step process. It is best to take one small step at a time. We often find that we slip back into our old ways, let habits overtake us. That's okay. The process of change sometimes feels overwhelming. Changing and growing takes time and forgiving. Forgive yourself first.

Knowing that we are the creators of our future is inspirational. When we give love, we get love. We produce a circle of love. When we understand this, we can place love's creation in the context of our life's work. When we care, we create love. When we understand another human being, we produce love. When we act with humility, we are able to appreciate the truth in life and see things as they are. This creates love. Inevitably, there is love in everything we do.

We need only take the first step in our journey with the commitment to honor ourselves. For in loving ourselves, we learn to share our kindness and gentleness with others. There is one simple truth—the love flows through you.

* * * * * * * *

God bless.

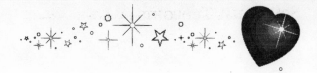

The human heart has hidden treasures.

—Charlotte Bronte

ABOUT THE AUTHOR

Paula Peisner Coxe was born in Los Angeles. She was educated at the University of California, Los Angeles and completed a Master's Degree in Business Administration at the University of Southern California. Ms. Coxe is a management consultant and the author of *Finding Time: Breathing Space for Women Who Do Too Much*, its companion journal, *Breathing Space*, and *Finding Peace: Letting Go and Liking It*. Paula lives and writes in Oregon with her husband and two daughters.

Also Available Are These Fine Business-Related Books From Sourcebooks—

Enjoy These Other Fine Books From Sourcebooks—

New From Sourcebooks!

365 Days Of Creative Play by Sheila Ellison and Judith Gray
The essential guide to a wide variety of creative projects for young children. This fantastic selection of indoor and outdoor activities will encourage your child's imagination, growth, and problem solving skills.

384 pages, ISBN: 1-57071-029-5 (lay-flat paperback) $12.95

365 Foods Kids Love To Eat by Sheila Ellison and Judith Gray
Finally, the cookbook parents have been waiting for! Filled with nutritious, kid-tested recipes, this cookbook will appeal to the whole family, especially those kids with finicky appetites.

416 pages, ISBN: 1-57071-030-9 (lay-flat paperback) $12.95

Random Acts: A Kindness Journal by the Editors of Conari Press
From the phenomenal bestseller *Random Acts of Kindness*, this journal will help you chronicle kindness in the world. A family memoir or a personal keepsake, *Random Acts* keeps the beauty of life's touching moments close to your heart.

160 pages, ISBN: 1-57071-034-1 (paperback) $7.95

Breathing Space: A Journal For Women Who Do Too Much
Let this elegant journal be the place where you find the peaceful time you deserve. Filled with quotes, inspirational suggestions, and tips from the best-selling *Finding Time*, by Paula Peisner Coxe. Celebrate your personal time!

160 pages, ISBN: 1-57071-036-8 (paperback) $7.95

The Small Business Marketing Guide by Ian Rosengarten
An A-Z guide to the tools and tactics of marketing your business. A must for any small business owner's library.

152 pages, ISBN: 1-57071-032-5 (paperback) $8.95

Great Idea! Now What? by Howard Bronson with Peter Lange
Turn your dreams into reality with help from the absolute best idea development book ever created. Learn how to develop, test, market, and sell your idea—without a huge financial risk. Discover your best ideas and act upon your dreams!

200 pages, ISBN: 1-57071-039-2 (paperback) $8.95

To order these terrific new books or to receive a catalog, call us at:

708-961-3900

Or write to:

Sourcebooks, Inc.
P.O. Box 372
Naperville, IL 60566